BREXIT'S A MUSICAL TRICK

NOT A TREAT

MIKE CASHMAN

with PETER COOK and ROBIN WALLINGTON

Published by ViewDelta Press
Paperback ISBN - 978-1-9162486-3-2
November 2020

Viewdelta BAMT202103221431
Produced in United Kingdom

Cover Design by Spiffing Covers

The Prologue

Do you hear what's happened here?
Are you concerned when people cheat?
Have you concluded on the evidence
That #BrexitsATrickNotATreat?
Do you recall how this played out?
And do you ask what Brexit's for?
#BrexitsAMusicalTrick,
As we shall now explore.

So, enjoy the presentation,
Which will all be done in song.
It isn't finished yet,
And so, we hope it's not too long.
If you have opinions,
Please tell us in case we are wrong!

Dedication

This book is dedicated to the public figures whose extraordinary actions give rise to so many opportunities for satire.

What, More Brexit Songs?

Yes - in two sections

- "**Brexit's a Musical Trick**" is a full-length satirical Musical covering events from early 2016 up to 2020.

  #BrexitsAMusicalTrick

  This features more than 40 new lyrics, together with five cases where a song that was in the earlier book "Brexit's a Trick not a Treat?" served the narrative purpose well with some minor changes.

- There is also a section (headed "**Brexit's Still A Trick Not a Treat?**") which more than 30 new songs triggered by events after the September 2019 unlawful proroguing - with one song about the alleged events leading up to a possible impeachment in another country.

  Misuse of power, misleading the electorate and political inconsistency are fruitful triggers for satire - a song declaring that the Government had fulfilled all its duties, following due process, is unlikely to raise a chuckle. Let's just say that this was a particularly fruitful period for these satirical songs.

For the songs in the last section, any dates shown are the dates on which I wrote the pieces concerned.

Our thanks and apologies of course are due to the very talented original writers and artists whose work was the further inspiration for this book.

The original lyrics (for each song that has been imitated) and recordings of it should be available online. For most songs the words here should match the tune exactly, so you should be able to karaoke them if you would like to. Occasionally there is an extra verse or two compared to the original.

Those who are looking for a politically neutral commentary should look elsewhere. The songs in this book do not take a kindly view of those who seek to mislead, and that leads us to be more critical of those who mislead more.

Material related to my earlier book can be found online by searching **#BrexitsATrickNotATreat.** The hashtag for this book is **#BrexitsAMusicalTrick.**

I welcome the contributions by Robin Wallington and Peter Cook, eminent in their own fields, with a clear talent for song parody too.

It was a great pleasure to sing an impromptu duet with Peter of "Bercow's Yellow Hammer" as we were at the European Commission in London in January 31st to say "Goodbye and Thank you".

In this new (January 2021) revision I have added Theryline's "On My Own" after "One Day More"., and I have included an additional final song to allow the country's leader and his assistant to give us their assessment of 2020 - "Failure Doesn't Matter in the Past" I have made space for these by moving a few songs to the next book ("I Don't Beg Pardon").

We have also in Summer 2020 been recording 24 songs from the Musical for CD and USB, in a socially-distanced manner, one singer at a time. We reassigned and revised some lines, in the light of what worked best when performing the songs. The CD or USB is of course the perfect way to enhance your enjoyment of this book, to hear 24 of the songs in the Musical performed by talented singers, with orchestral accompaniment. And there is one poem about a "Wise Lady" too.

I hope that this book informs and amuses you. We would love you to review the book and/or CD, for example on Amazon or social media, or just feedback to info@viewdelta.com

Thank you

Mike Cashman, January 2021

Contents

Brexit's A Musical Trick - In 3 Acts

Prologue

Act 1 - Camerine

Act 2 – Theryline

Act 3 – Boris ValBoris

The action takes place in an imaginary country which is considering a Brexit from the European Union after a referendum on the subject.

A Synopsis of the Three Acts and Notes on the Musical may be found following Act 3.

Brexit's A Musical Trick – Cast

The cast is shown here in order of appearance. The underlined characters appear in many scenes; the other characters in general have much smaller singing parts (fewer solo singing appearances), which gives scope for doubling up some characters.

GRIEVOUS ....is an MP who introduces the story.
BORIS VALBORIS ...struggles with the injustice of not being Prime Minister.
CAMERINE.............surprisingly became Prime Minister twice, but was unsure of how to govern a country, and so fell into the habit of holding referenda so that the People could govern instead.
STURGINE..............wants to be Prime Minister of her own country.
EOIAUN MACSTAY BLACKSCOT_ Lord Off the Aisles.
LAUNDRETTE LEADSOM .....tried to become Prime Minister and thought she should be Prime Minister because of being a mother.
GOVERT................didn't want to become Prime Minister but changed his mind when he decided the others were all worse.
THERYLINE.............is a strong and stable character. Concerned to ensure that she can be Prime Minister.
REES-MOGGI ....lies in the House of Commons
FARAGIER ....sought to ensure that his country never left the European Union so that he could continue his career complaining about it.
WIDDY FARAGIER...... despite her name, is not Faragier's widow, because that would mean he was dead.
PANNINI ....is a Lordly Lawyer; don't panic.

EADIDI .... is an opposing lawyer.
SUPREME COURT JUDGE .....is already Supreme
TUSKER................. is the elephant in the room.
CROSBI.................. works out who to blame
ARLINE.................. helps Prime Minister to stay as Prime Minister.
CORBOCHE .... irrepressible street urchin who hasn't worked out how to become Prime Minister.
THE QUEEN........... of the country - sacks Prime Ministers when necessary (so we're told).
The LEDBYDONKEYS team (WILLEAU, JAMESONNE, BENNI, OLLYVERT)
.... Embarrass most of the other characters by reminding them what they said.
DAVIDE DAVINE.... wouldn't mind being Prime Minister if someone else did all the work.
GAVINI .... carries in the man who wants to be the next Prime Minister
CUNNINGS............ tells the Prime Minister what to do.

The CHORUS often represent VOTERS/ PEOPLE of different types, and also sometimes the TORINES, their BACKERS, the ERGINES, the DUPINES, the LABOUR SUPORTERS or the EUNIES
VOTERS................. know what they're voting for.
TORINES .... support all the Prime Ministers in this musical. Or not.
ERGINES .... tell the Prime Minister what to do.
DUPINES............... is a group of MPs with votes for sale; tell the Prime Minister what to do.
TORINE BACKERS ... tell the Prime Minister what to do.
LABOUR SUPPORTERS...can't tell the Prime Minister what to do
EUNIES.................. wonder what the Prime Minister is doing.

Brexits A Musical Trick – Act 1 (Camerine)

Prologue

Inspired by: *"Do You Hear the People Sing?"*

Enter the MP GRIEVOUS:

GRIEVOUS (to audience)

Do you hear what's happened here?
Are you concerned when people cheat?
Have you concluded on the evidence
That #BrexitsATrickNotATreat?
Do you recall how this played out?
And do you ask what Brexit's for?
#BrexitsAMusicalTrick,
As we shall now explore.

So, enjoy the presentation,
Which will all be done in song.
It isn't finished yet,
And so, we hope it's not too long.
If you have opinions,
Please tell us in case we are wrong!

WHOLE COMPANY ENTER & JOIN IN, singing the words as above again with GRIEVOUS.

All exit except VOTERS,

Look Round – Austerity

Inspired by: *Look Down*

VOTERS (all)

Look round, look round,
Austerity is why.
Look round, look round,
You're poor until you die.
The cuts are strong.
Facilities are gone.
Look round, look round,
There's nothing going on.

VOTER 1

I've done no wrong,
I lost my job then but
I tried so long.
My benefits are cut.

VOTER 2

I will not shirk
I haven't lost my powers.
I look for work.
There's only "zero hours".

VOTER 3

I'll go berserk
When I get work
With some pay.

VOTERS (All)
Look round, look round,
Austerity is why.
How long must we
Have no share of the pie?
Look down, look down,
You are the lowest rank
Look down, look down,
And visit the food bank
All exit.

Do or Die?

Inspired by: *"Who am I"*

Enter BORIS VALBORIS, making notes in a notebook.

BORIS VALBORIS:
They think I will Remain,
And then we will advance.
But I think it is plain;
This bid could be my chance.
Why should I do what's right,
And back the cause that's true?
When I could lead the fight
To depart from EU?

If I speak, I am adored.
If I stay silent, I'll be bored.

I am the darling of thousands of voters, who all hate Remain.
Can I abandon them?
How would they cope without me to campaign?

If I speak, I am adored.
If I stay silent, I'll be bored.

Do or die?
Can I accept my fate as not PM?

Sit only on that old back bench again?
These charlatans who speak for go,
Who need my help and my ego,
Do or die?
Can I conceal the truth from everyone,
And lead this gang until the vote is done?
And must the cause I did decry
Be just my cause though there's no "why"?
Must I lie?

GOVERT and CAMERINE enter and listen
BORIS VALBORIS continues:
How can I work this so my ratings rise?
How will I give the world a big surprise?
My heart belongs to lies I know;
I made that judgement long ago
It got me sacked from many jobs;
But I don't care for snowflake sobs.

(Notices GOVERT)
Do or die? Do or die?
Boris redone!
And so Govert you see I'll do
Whatever act to Leave EU
Do or die?
Who'll more fix this one? *(All exit)*

Look Round - Voting

VOTERS enter and pace around the stage throughout this song, forming and re-forming the groupings that sing the lines.
This has been written for a group of 6 Voters, but could easily be adapted for only 4 Voters or for a larger group. The initial lines are sung by all voters, the following lines by different smaller groups, and the final lines by a majority group.

Inspired by: *Look Down*

VOTERS (ALL)
Look round, look round.
And now I get my say.
I must decide.
How I will vote today.

VOTERS 1 & 2
I heard them say
Why I should vote Remain.
If I do that,
I don't know what I gain.

VOTERS 5 and 6
EU is fine.
Sometimes you take the mick.
And some will whine.
Let's give them all a kick.

VOTERS 3 AND 4
Look round, look round.
Should we defend our shores?
VOTERS 2 and 6
But have we found

That we have no more wars.

VOTERS 4 AND 5
There are experts
Betting their shirts
On Remain.

VOTERS 3 AND 6
From Middle East
They're sending more and more.
VOTERS 1, 3 AND 6
I think at least
That we should close the door.

VOTERS 1 4 AND 5
And every week,
Three fifty million less.
VOTERS 1,4,5 and 6
Which we could seek
To fund the NHS.

Other VOTERS enter and form 4 groups, VOTERS 1 to 6 from the previous song are all within groups A and B.
Enter GOVERT, LAUNDRETTE, CAMERINE, GRIEVOUS, CUNNINGS, FARAGIER, WIDDY, REES-MOGGI, and DAVID DAVINE who join relevant groups as seen below.
Enter CORBOCHE, wo in the next song should wander curiously from group to group, ending up in Group D, but not singing, except for the last line.
Enter THERYLINE, who stands near Group D bit does not sing, except for the last line.
[NOTE: If cast numbers are small then omit these characters from this song]

We Know What We're Voting For

Inspired by: *'Do You Hear the People Sing?*

THE PEOPLE: GROUP A – *with GOVERT & LAUNDRETTE*
Do you hear that we're concerned?
In fact, we're absolutely sick
Of being analysed and patronised,
Despised and told we're thick?
Well now at last we've got a vote.
So just for once we've got the stick,
Giving the Government
A bit of a forceful kick.
What on earth is going to happen, when we hit the exit door?
We're ready for some changes, yes, we're absolutely sure.
We're sure of this, we know what we're voting for.

THE PEOPLE: - GROUP C – *including REES-MOGGI & DAVID DAVINE*
Do you hear that we're concerned?
In fact, we're absolutely sick
Of the rules and regulations
Making the Single Market tick.
And they're stopping Tax Avoidance.
If you skip tax, you're in the nick.
Time to give markets
A somewhat disruptive kick.
And we know what then will happen, when we hit the exit door?
We're ready for some changes, yes, we're absolutely sure.
We're sure of this, we know what we're voting for

THE PEOPLE: GROUP D – *including GRIEVOUS. CAMERINE, and STURGENE*

Do you hear that we're concerned?
In fact, we're absolutely sick
Of the lies and misdirection.
Do they think we all are thick?
There are lies upon a bus,
Though their posters are so slick.
It's not a treat,
It's just a very nasty trick.
What on earth is going to happen, when we hit the exit door?
We're dreading all the changes, are we absolutely sure?
So sure of this, to know what we're voting for?

THE PEOPLE: - GROUP B – *including FARAGIER, WIDDY and CUNNINGS*

Do you hear that we're concerned?
In fact, we're absolutely sick
Of the queues, exasperations
You can't get in unless you're quick,
For the places in the schools,
And of the jobs they get the pick.
Time to give Government
A bit of a forceful kick.
And we're glad that this will happen, when we hit the exit door.
We're ready for some changes, yes, we're absolutely sure.
We're sure of this, we know what we're voting for.

In this completion of the song, all groups repeat their verse, singing simultaneously, They march together for the first 2 lines, then split up into different areas of the stage, with Groups A, B and C coming together again for the last 3 lines, marching to finish at the front of the stage on the final line, while Group D are on their own but parallel.

A – with GOVERT & LAUNDRETTE	**B – including FARAGIER, WIDDY and CUNNINGS**
Do you hear that we're concerned?	
In fact, we're absolutely sick	
Of being analysed and patronised	Of the queues, exasperations
Despised and told we're thick?	You can't get in unless you're quick,
Well now at last we've got a vote,	For the places in the schools
So just for once we've got the stick,	And of the jobs they get the pick,
Giving the Government	Time to give Government
A bit of a forceful kick,	A bit of a forceful kick,
What on earth is going to happen, when we hit the exit door?	And we're glad that this will happen, when we hit the exit door,
We're ready for some changes, yes, we're absolutely sure.	
We're sure of this, we know what we've voting for	

In this completion of the song, all groups repeat their verse, singing simultaneously, They march together for the first 2 lines, then split up into different areas of the stage, with Groups A, B and C coming together again for the last 3 lines, marching to finish at the front of the stage on the final line, while Group D are on their own but parallel.

C – including REES-MOGGI and DAVID DAVINE	**D – including GRIEVOUS. CAMERINE & STURGENE**
Do you hear that we're concerned?	
In fact, we're absolutely sick	
Of the rules and regulations	Of the lies and misdirection.
Making the Single Market tick,	Do they think we all are thick?
And they're stopping Tax Avoidance;	There are lies upon a bus.
If you skip tax, you're in the nick,	Though their posters are so slick,
Time to give markets	It's not a treat,
A somewhat disruptive kick,	It's just a very nasty trick,
And we know what then will happen, when we hit the exit door,	What on earth is going to happen, if we hit the exit door?
We're ready for some changes, yes, we're absolutely sure,	We're dreading all the changes, are we absolutely sure?
We're sure of this, we know what we've voting for,	So sure of this, to know what we've voting for?

(All exit)

Now Bring Referendum Twenty-Sixteen On

Inspired by: *Now Bring Me Prisoner 24601*

Enter CAMERINE and VALBORIS in discussion
CAMERINE:
Now bring referendum twenty-sixteen on.
My coalition with the Lib Dems is gone.
You know what that means?

VALBORIS:
Yes, it means you're free.

CAMERINE:
So, it means you get
Your chance to support me now.
You want Remain.

VALBORIS:
I think I might go Leave.

CAMERINE:
You don't think that.

VALBORIS:
If I don't then I'll grieve.
My thinking is that Leave will lose.
But I'll be soaring.

CAMERINE:
I'll be sore again,
Unless you back Remaining, just like George

VALBORIS:
I've thought Remaining for some 19 years.

Or maybe I will Leave.

CAMERINE
Eight years as London mayor,
The rest writing for the Telegraph -
Mostly for a laugh.

VALBORIS:
I'm declaring Boris ValBoris.

CAMERINE
Well I'm Remain.
I will regret your move.
I will regret this
Choice, Boris ValBoris.
(Both exit)

Brexitian Fantasy

Inspired by: *Bohemian Rhapsody?*

Enter VOTERS

VOTER1:
Is this the real thing?
Is this just fantasy?
Caught in a Farage
Escaped from reality,
Open your eyes
Look out for the lies and see.
VOTER2:
I'm just a voter, I need no clarity,
Because I'm EC done, EC go,
Boris high, sterling low,
Any way the pound goes, doesn't really matter to me, to me.

VOTER3:
Brexit, just stuffed the pound,
Got the rumour posted live,
Let the currency just dive.
Brexit, we were getting there,
But then we went and threw it all away.
VOTER4:
Britain, ooh-ooh-ooh
Didn't mean to make you cry.
If we're not afloat again this time tomorrow
Carry on, carry on, as if nothing really matters.

VOTER 5:
Too late, we blew it all.
Sent shivers down my spine.
ValBoris on the line.

Goodbye, economy, now got to go,
Gotta leave you all behind and face the truth.
Britain, ooh-ooh-ooh
Did we want to go?
I sometimes wish no referendum at all.

VOTERS 1-5:
I see a little fantasy of a plan,
Boris now, Boris how, do you have a plandango?
Fantasy financial, Very insubstantial
Oh Govert, oh ValBoris,
In procession to Brecession,
Oh, ValBoris and his Tories
And their stories,

Enter EUNIES
VOTER1:
Now we're a poor state, not much we're earning,
EUNIES
They're just a poor state, took the wrong turning.
Spare them and let them back into this EC,
VOTERS 1-5
Oh, we voted out back then, will you let us in
Again?

EUNIES	VOTERS
No, we will not let you in.	Let us in! Oh please?
No, we will not let you in.	Let us in! Just once?
No, we will not let you in.	Let us in,
Will not let you in.	(Let us in!)

EUNIES:
Never, never let you in

Never let you back in, oh.
No, no, no, no, no, no, no.
VOTERS:
Oh, mama mia, mama mia (Mama mia, let me in.)
Boris, Govert have no plan put aside for me, for me, for me.

EUNIES:
So, you think you can leave us and have the same trade?
So, you think it's like you're in if you haven't paid?
Oh, you guys, should have thought of this June 2016,
When all that you said was "just gotta get right outta here".
(Oh, ooh, oh ooh)

VOTERS
Nothing really matters,
Except sovereignty,
Nothing really matters,
Nothing really matters to me.
Any way the wind blows.
(All exit)

Hasty Referendum

Inspired by: *Valjean Arrested & Forgiven*
ENTER BLACKSCOT, STURGINE, LAUNDRETTE, GOVERT, REES-MOGGI, GRIEVOUS, VALBORIS, FARAGIER, CUNNINGS and CAMERINE.
They may be looking at TV monitors showing results.

BLACKSCOT
Hold a hasty referendum,
With two options on the card.

GOVERT

There are rules but we can bend 'em,

BLACKSCOT
Well it cannot be that hard.

GRIEVOUS:
Leave campaign from the beginning
Made some claims that were not right.

REES-MOGGI
But it seems the scores show winning
For the Leave team?

GOVERT
That is right.

BLACKSCOT
But now Dave you left so early,
Something surely slipped your mind?
You forgot implementation.
Would you leave this task behind?

CAMERINE
Oh, I cannot be the captain.
Maybe Boris will say "Yes".
Or some other crazy Leaver
For a Titanic success.

And remember this my Party -
Now is time to end the fight.
My response, sincere and hearty -
Tories all must now unite.

It is now the time to barter.
You must no more now be vexed.
Yes, I've been your Brexit martyr.
My successor will be next.

All exit except GOVERT, VALBORIS AND LAUNDRETTE. GOVERT and VALBORIS are Centre Stage and LAUNDRETTE is watching from the side.

A Man Such as You

Inspired by: *Confrontation*

GOVERT
Boris, at last,
And this just makes me sad,
Throughout your past,
You mess things up so bad

VALBORIS
Before you think of splitting, Govert,
Before you give up on my campaign,
Listen to me. I think that I'll still lead.
I was supposed to send a tweet,
Promising a reward job to Laundrette,
And it's true I haven't done it yet,
But I'll do that, get her support,
But I'll do that ...

GOVERT
Do you think I'm mad?
I've worked with you across the years.
A man such as you can never change.
A man such as you.

VALBORIS
Think of me what you like.
There is a speech that I said I'd write.
I did not write it last night,
Tried again when had some sleep.
In it I'll almost get things right.
Just give me time to get this writing done.
I am telling you Govert,
Let me try, I think you should.
I have always wanted power,
And my speech will be so good.
I am telling you, Govert,
This I say with all my heart. -
I will try to lead the team.
Yes, I will do my part.

GOVERT
Men like you can never change.
Men like you can never change.
No Boris ValBoris.
My duty's to the cause.
You've messed this up,
Give up now, Boris ValBoris.
Now the time has come for me.
Boris bid will crash and burn.
You should leave the contest now.
It is time for Govert's turn.
You had chance to make your pitch.
Disappointed Laundrette too.
If you cannot write a speech,
Then there is no hope for you.

VALBORIS
And now it seems to me today

GOVERT
You should stand down and let me run.

VALBORIS
You have a point, I must withdraw.

GOVERT
I think that's right just as you say

VALBORIS
You'll get the leadership now done.

GOVERT
I've no charisma but I'll score.

GOVERT and LAUNDRETT Exit opposite directions

What Have I Done?

Inspired by: *What Have I Done?*

BORIS VALBORIS
What have I done,
ValBoris, what have I done?
I had to tweet my support
For Laundrette Leadsom
So that she'd join my side,
But the time got so late
That no time was left,
And no speech on my plate,
The speech to be king which nobody hears;
Here's where I stand after all these deprived years.

If there is ever a chance to lead,
I said that this is the chance that I need.
My life was a void with an injustice vile -
I've not been Prime Minister all of this while.
I've been mistreated, missed out and beaten,
Since I didn't get captain of Eton.

Yet why did I not write my speech,
And send the tweet and help Govert?
He treated me like any Leader.
He gave me support.
He called me "Leaver".
This was my chance to claim my prize,
And no one laughed.

To be Prime Minister at last,
But up the wall my chance I've spaffed.

Take a tweet for a treat.
Be the PM at last.
This is all I have lived for -
To make sense of my past.

One speech from me and I was in,
To number 10 with no more sin
Instead I bungled the whole shit show.
I should be Prime Minister even so.
Govert has said I could not lead.
How does he know?
Why won't I get to number 10?
There is no other way to go.

I am stumbling and I fall,
And announce I cannot stand.
And it's been unfair again;
I have lost by Govert's hand.
What can I get from this mess,
As my leadership bid wrecks?
Well perhaps I'll get a chance
To be the best of foreign secs.

Brexit's A Musical Trick – Act 2 (Theryline)

Enter TORINES & REES-MOGGI with GOVERT, VALBORIS, LAUNDRETTE and THERYLINE

At the End of The Day We Have Need of a Leader

Inspired by: *At the End of The Day*

GOVERT
At the end of the day we have need of a leader

GOVERT shoves VALBORIS out
GOVERT & TORINES
And Boris is out, he has messed up his chance,
It's a puzzle. It's a mess.
And there's no one that you would call gallant,
There are more rounds, we have to vote,
Can you say yes,
With this lack of good talent?

GOVERT
At the end of the day we have need of a leader,

TORINES
And the Fox and the Crabbe have been washed down the drain,
Well Govert said he would manage,
He's already seen off ValBoris,

LAUNDRETTE shoves GOVERT out
But Govert has slid out of the race, and there's only two left,
To deal with the damage

LAUNDRETTE:
At the end of the day I'm the one who's the mother.
So, you should vote for me, taking this to account.
What do you say? Then I'm banned?
Well I think that's the harshest reaction.
There's some anger in this land,
Referendum will still need some action,
And someone will have to pay
At the end of the day.

All except THERYLINE *withdraw to the edge of the Stage leaving* THERYLINE *centre Stage*

THERYLINE
They sent for me today now it's my poisoned chalice.
I showed slightly Remain but it's now time to Leave.

TORINES
There are voters back at home,
And the voters must be appeased.
And you're lucky to be our leader,
And are you pleased?

REES-MOGGI
Are you sending them notice?

TORINES
Have you seen how the hate crime
Is on the increase?
There's a mood in the country,
Intolerance now.
It's up to you Theryline
To make this thing cease?

REES-MOGGI
Send article 50,
And send it them now!
And the Daily Mail's waiting.
For they want us to leave the EC.
Theryline better look out
to keep them sweet
And it will not be easy.

THERYLINE is trying to look important by brandishing her ring-binder and pen.

TORINES
At the end of the day then we've got a new leader.
Will MPs in Parliament follow her lead?
Send the notice. Send it soon.
Some thought that we should go the day after,
Wanted millions to help with our health.
Some thought nothing could ever be dafter.
Well you gotta get-away
At the end of the day.

What Have We Here, Oh You Closet Remainer?

Inspired by: *What Have We Here Little Innocent Sister?*

REES-MOGGI
And what have we here, oh you closet Remainer?
(Grabs paper from Theryline ring-binder)
Theryline tell us all, oh this we beseech?
"I should now make it plain,
That it's best to Remain."
Now you think you can reign?
It's a hell of a speech!

Enter GRIEVOUS

THERYLINE
Give me that speech back!

GRIEVOUS
What is this dispute all about?
Will someone clarify the row?
This is a Party not a caucus.
Now come on, MPs, settle down;
A Point of Order to dispute
Leave is the only game in town
Can some committee sort this out?
And be as open as you can.
(GRIEVOUS exits)

VALBORIS
Now someone say how this began

REES-MOGGI
At the end of the day,
She's the one who began it.

There's a speech that she made when
She went for Remain.
There's a doubt about her beliefs.
You can guess that she still backs Remaining.
You can bet she'll soften the Deal;
That's very plain.
And I know we won't like it.

THERYLINE
Well it's true that I spoke, and I spoke as Remainer,
But I thought at that time
That the Leave team would lose.
Now I've moved to the Leave gang,
And no-one should grieve
And no-one should fret
Please accept my excuse.

TORINES
Till the end of the day
We'll be watching her closely.
We'll be watching her moves,
And be watching her talks.
While we're hoping for our Brexit,
She's the one in negotiation;
You must reinforce her muscles;
We gotta have implementation;
She must be ready for tussles
With Brussels.

REES-MOGGI
I might have known we'd get Remain.
I might have seen the poisoned clause.
I might have guessed your little secret.

Ah yes, the convert Theryline,
Who keeps herself so Leave and clean,
You'd be the problem if we're late.
We heard you at Lancaster Gate.

THERYLINE
I think you're being very mean
I'll get things done, trust Theryline

TORINES
Just do it

THERYLINE
I'll negotiate with them
So poker-faced, cunning.
There is no
Comment'ry running.

REES-MOGGI
Well we'll back her today.
TORINES
Back her today.

REES-MOGGI
Right my girl. On your way.
All exit.

Lovely Tax Breaks

Inspired by: *Lovely Ladies*

Enter TORINE BACKERS *&* REES-MOGGI

REES-MOGGI
I smell tax breaks,
Tax breaks in U.K.
And the other territories.
It's Paradise today.
Lovely tax-breaks,
Which the EU lacks.
Where's the opportunity
To never pay your tax.
Tax evaders like to hide the facts.

Enter THERYLINE

REES-MOGGI
Lovely tax breaks
Waiting for the smash,
Waiting for the customers
Who move a lot of cash.
Lovely tax-breaks;
We are on your side.
If you think tax owing
Then there's places you can hide.
Gaping loopholes that are open wide!

REES-MOGGI
Come here my dear
Let's see the Deal we fear,
This withdrawal.

THERYLINE
Redlines, I'll show them to you!

REES-MOGGI
Just get us out.

THERYLINE
We'll need transition time too!

REES-MOGGI
Just get us out.
It's up to you.

THERYLINE
I'll take two years.

BACKER
We've not got time.
That is too lax.
My dear we all must dodge our tax.

REES-MOGGI
Lovely tax breaks
Tax breaks in U.K
EU tax avoidance checks
Will never be OK.
Lovely tax-breaks
Which the EU lacks.
Where's the opportunity
To never pay your tax?
Tax evaders like to hide the facts.

BACKER *(to THERYLINE)*
What clever funds.
Your clever husband's got one.
What luck you've got.
Do well in Cayman my dear.
I'll back the lot.

THERYLINE
Don't say that. Leave us alone

REES-MOGGI *(whispers)*
Trust your MPs

REES-MOGGI
Let's make a guess.
I think he's Capital Group, just think of that.

THERYLINE
It pays the bills.

BACKER
Just think of that.

THERYLINE
What can I do? I'll make the Bill.
Our coffers fill

BACKERS (This verse is omitted in "film" version)
Lovely tax breaks,
Tax breaks in U.K.
EU tax avoidance checks
Will never be OK.

Lovely tax-breaks,
Which the EU lacks.
Where's the opportunity
To never pay your tax?
Tax evaders like to hide the facts.

BACKER
Gimme the facts. That's their leader, yes?

BACKER2
She wears brown pants.
Gets us out of this mess.
She's got a man,
Got his funds in Cayman.

BACKER1
I might have known.
Always some offshore plan.
Lovely tax-breaks, come along and join us.
Lovely tax-breaks

REES-MOGGI *(spoken)*
Tax breaks we must advance
"No Deal" gives us our best chance.

REES-MOGGI
Come on dearie, why all this fuss?
You're no cleaner than the rest of us.
Life has put you on the summit of the heap.
Join your colleagues.
Make money in your sleep.
That's right, dearie.

You invest the lot.
That's right dearie,
Show 'em what you've got.

Onshore, offshore, assets every class,
Make a lot of money while you're sitting on your arse
Rich folk, rich folk, leaders of the land.
See them with investments and you see their future's planned.
All it takes is, say, nine fifty grand.
Lovely tax-breaks,
UK is so lax.
Got a lot of income,
But there's not a lot of tax.

THERYLINE
Well that's one thing, but if there's a Deal.
We will need transition time with EU rules, I feel.
Easy Money, I see the appeal.
EU Tax Avoidance rules will catch us all for real.
(Exit THERYLINE)

REES-MOGGI & BACKERS *(to each other)*
Don't you know,
That we may need
To push for a No Deal.
All exit.

There is a Deal That Can Be Done

Inspired by: *There Is A Castle on a Cloud*

Enter THERYLINE, who sings in a reverie.

THERYLINE

There is a deal that can be done.
I dream about that cherry pick.
I'd like to do that deal so quick,
My deal, so from EU we'll run.

I'll with a title Boris fob.
I will make Boris Foreign Sec.
But I'm afraid my Deal he'd wreck.
Davide and Fox must do the job.

Negotiation now can start.
We'll do the business by and by.
No comment'ry
While I run the show.
I'll say "Trust me", and I'll fix how we go.

I know they think that I'm Remain.
I'll have to show I'm very hard.
Then those Leavers won't be sick,
Not in my clever cherry pick.

Exit THERYLINE.

Master of the Spiel

Inspired by: *Master of the House*

ENTER FARAGIER & WIDDY, & TORINES/ERGINEs who watch this performance

FARAGIER
Hallo, dear folk.
You can trust me.
I'll do the work
To leave the EC.
There are countries
Do fine outside;
Norway is one.
Enjoy the ride.
Though you must beware
That it is not fair
To let into this joint
Folk to breaking point.

Master of the spiel,
Cracking awful jokes,
Appealing to the Far Right
Who are mostly blokes.
I will drink a pint,
I will smoke a cig,
So you know to trust me,
And my Brexit gig.

UKIP says we should be Leavers.
But we've argued with Vote Leave.
But something based on nothing
Might mean there's nothing to achieve.

She has sent the note,
Notice that we'll go;
But we won't agree
With others in this show.
Worrying the troops
In some nasty plights
Picking up their votes
When they're afraid of frights.
Everybody loves a Brexit.
Everybody is my friend.
I do whatever pleases,
Wheezes to bleed 'em in the end,

FARAGIER & ERGINES
Master of the spiel.
Quick to start some spin.
Always wants a floating vote
To float right in.
Calling to the poor,
Ally of the posh.
Poundshop Enoch Powell
With a load of dosh.
Everybody's normal bloke friend,

Everybody's headline man,

FARAGIER
But just look at the headlines.
Redlines? Mine were never in the plan.

FARAGIER
Enter, voter,
Turn on TV.
Just grab your pint,
And then look at me.
News is a curse.
Let's simplify.
Make you fear worse.
And pass on a lie.
Here the spin is spun.
Here the lies begun.
And here we have our fun,
Till the vote is won.

Lies beyond a joke.
Lies without relief.
Mix it with a bit of truth
To build belief.
Poster of a crowd.
Fears of a crush.
Filling up the airwaves
With a load of mush.

Candidates can all be welcome.
Though some seats are occupied.
Easy cheap subscriptions,
That you pay if you're on our side.

Pay into the fund.
That so many shunned.
Paying for the posters that had Britain stunned.

And the pound I'll short
Deal of a sort.
Not exactly legal but I'll escape Court.
When it comes to fixing markets,
There's the news and tweet to use.
All the little tit bits,
All the little shit bits,
Boris – with power you can abuse.

FARAGIER & ERGINES
Master of the spiel.
Quick to start some spin.
Always wants a floating vote
To float right in.
Calling to the poor
Ally of the posh.
Poundshop Enoch Powell

With a load of dosh.
Everybody's normal bloke
friend,
Everybody's headline man

FARAGIER
But just look at the voters.
Floaters? We'll get them if
we can.

WIDDY FARAGIER
I used to think
That I would learn to rule
But, hell's pyjamas,
Look I am now with this
fool.

Master of the spiel,
He can talk for real
Spilling out his claptrap,
How he wants a Deal.
Cunning coated prat,
Powell from the past;
Thinks he is a strategist
But doesn't last.
What a talking coat we see
here.
Leads us all to who knows
where.
But you see I've lasted,
Working with this bastard as
a pair.

FARAGIER & ERGINES
Master of the spiel.

WIDDY FARAGIER
Whom I will "adore".

FARAGIER & ERGINES
Master of No Deal.

WIDDY FARAGIER
Well, you have the floor.

FARAGIER & ERGINES
Master of the pint.
Smoker of the cig.

WIDDY FARAGIER
So you know to trust him
And his Brexit gig.

FARAGIER & ERGINES
Everybody bless our Brexit.
Everybody thinks it's real.

FARAGIER
Everybody raise a glass.
Raise it up Remainers' arse
ALL
Everybody raise a glass
To the master of the spiel.

Exit all.

Can the PM Give Our Rights Away?

Inspired by: *Waltz of Treachery*

Enter GOVERT, THERYLINE, GRIEVOUS, PANNINI and EADIDI

GOVERT
What to do?
What to say?
Can the PM
Give our rights away?

It's for her,
When she sees right,
To give notice,
Then our future's bright.

How can we
Need anyone else?
But PM
With notice she tells,

GRIEVOUS
But Gina
Speaks her cause.
Parliament -
It makes the laws.

Government
Can't please itself.
And leave MPs
Stuck on the shelf.

PANNINI QC
Your pleadings have some merit, now,
And I will take the briefing on.
Let us not say PM can do this deed.
It's Parliament, are we agreed?

EADIDI QC
That would be, who would say.
When domestic ruling's at play.
Here we see, this is meaty
But it's still international treaty.
Precedents teach us a lesson.
The Prime Minister has full discretion.

High Court can't
End the case.
Supreme Court is the
Decisive place.

PANNINI & EADIDI
Answers now
Must be sought.
So, let us all
Go to Supreme Court.

Enter SUPREME JUDGE who sits down and PANNINI and EADIDI stand before her. All others watch behind them.

Then the Court
States the case.

SUPREME JUDGE
"Bill of Rights
Governs this place".

"Brexit would
Reduce our rights.
That's not in
Executive's sights.
Parliament
Needs to vote.
On this judgement
All parties take note"

Exit all

Knowing Me Knowing EU

Inspired by: *Knowing Me Knowing You*

Enter THERYLINE, *with a letter.*
TUSKER *also enters, but stays in the sidelines until "Knowing me knowing eu", when he advances to be more visible, and listens with interest.*
Optionally, TUSKER *can sing the words in parentheses.*

THERYLINE
No more tax-free exports.
No more words from experts.
Got the bill straight through the house
Without a dent.
Then the note with article
Fifty was sent.

Knowing me, knowing eu (ah-haa),
Forty-eight, fifty-two.
Knowing me, knowing eu (ah-haa),
We just have to face it, this time we're through
This time we're through, time we're through, we're really through.
Breaking treaties with the EC, I know but we have to go
*(*TUSKER *shakes his head sadly)*
We have to go this time,
We have to go, this time we know.
Knowing me, knowing eu,
It's the best we can do.

No more EC orders.
No more easy borders.
In these old familiar places,
Farage would play.
Now there's just two years before
Going away.

Knowing me, knowing eu (ah-haa),
There is nothing we can do.
Knowing me, knowing eu (ah-haa),
We just have to hand the control to eu.
(TUSKER nods)
Control to you, control to you.
This time it's true, we're really through.
Breaking treaties with the EC I know but we have to go.
We have to go this time,
Two years we go, that time I know.
Knowing me, knowing eu,
It's the best we can do.

What I would like, real now.
Cherry pick our deal now.
But you said we can't do that.
(TUSKER shakes his head)
That's such a shame.
Now we're got 2 years, that's all.
Who can we blame?
Knowing me, knowing eu (ah-haa),
There is nothing we can do.
Knowing me, knowing eu (ah-haa),
We just have to hand the control to eu,
Control to you, control to you.
This time it's true, we're really through.
On security I made threats I know, but we have to go,
(TUSKER nods)
We have to go this time,
Two years we go, that time I know.
Knowing me, knowing eu,
It's the best we can do.

Response to Article 50

Inspired by: *I Will Survive*

TUSKER

At first, we were not worried, thought you had it planned,
Till the Tory party argument got out of hand;
And then they made a crazy fuss upon a bus that was so long,
And no-one heard the experts say this bus was simply wrong.
And so, you're out – you've made your case.
I just walked in to find there's Theryline with Number Fifty Face.
Your referendum had no lock
Or threshold to make it through,
And so now you've chosen Brexit

THERYLINE

Forty-eight to fifty-two.

(THERYLINE nods)

TUSKER

Go, now go. And shut the door.
Negotiate your trade deals, we won't do them any more.
Weren't you the ones that always said just how you feel?
Well now please do not imagine
You can cherry-pick your deal.
Oh no, not now!
That is not how.
As long as you will live,
You're on your own, that's starting now.
We're united twenty-seven.
This may not quite be heaven,
But, according to our shout,
We'd say it's better in than out, hey, hey.

So, you talked about three hundred fifty millions?
I think you'll find an exit bill in billions.
And you spent so many days just thinking what was your way out.
We used to worry for UK, but now EU goes on without.
Now see EC – running EU.
Dear colleagues we are sorry but we'll manage without you.
And so, you felt like having opt-outs,
And you'd argue all the night,
So, we're saving all our treaties for the ones who'll treat us right.

Go, now go. And shut the door.
Negotiate your trade deals, we won't do them any more.
Weren't you the ones who said it's better out than in?
Do you think you'll get a better deal?
You really think you'll win?
Oh, that's not true. And now you're through.
You followed Govert and ValBoris, and that Faragier crew.
When they have gone away, you'll have tariffs all to pay
You may survive. But will you thrive?
Exit TUSKER

I Saw the Polls (Stable and Strong)

Inspired by: *I Saw Him Once*

THERYLINE
Stable and strong,
I can't be wrong.
I don't need debates to say
That I am the leader of us today.
The leader who's emerging for this task.
Now people, really vote for me I ask.

I walk alone. Like Maggie T. that's me.
Can she have known her advent to my destiny?
I had to run again,
And thus, fulfil my dream.
I saw the polls.
My lead was true.
I saw my goals,
To leave EU.

In My Life

Inspired by: *In My Life*

THERYLINE
In my life
I have much that I need
I have Boris and Govert too.
Enter VALBORIS and GOVERT on this line
But my lead, that small lead
In my eyes it is just not enough
To legislate through.

No more Bills
No more, now the votes must be penned.
My heart fills
With the hope that the ills of our time can end.

In debates, I'll be silent and stable and strong -
And I'm sure that they'll buy it.
Yes indeed
This election will top
As if something is over
The strength of the quiet.
Exit VALBORIS and GOVERT

In debates,
There'll be someone who doesn't take part,

Who is able,
Strong and stable.

A Poll Full of Votes

Inspired by: *A Heart Full of Love*

Enter CROSBI

CROSBI

A poll full of votes -
The lead won't last long,
She's doing everything all wrong,
Oh, who to blame?

THERYLINE

I am the one who lost this game,
Dear Party folk,
I've screwed up - that's no joke.

CROSBI

A poll full of votes,

CROSBI & THERYLINE

A lead that won't float;

Enter ARLINE who watches them both

CROSBI

Our plan was foolish but it's true.
Ah shit! Ah shit!!
And now we're staring in the pit.

THERYLINE

Who will vote?

CROSBI

Who will lead?

THERYLINE

A poll full of votes.

The lead won't last long

CROSBI
You know he's waiting
For his chance,
Waiting for you.

THERYLINE
Not just yet.

CROSBI
What we need.

CROSBI& THERYLINE
This is just a bad dream.
We must be D.U.P.'d.

ARLINE

This was always yours to lose.
You'll regret you ever
Asked for votes.

Now to work with us
You have to choose,
With your notes,

Ask for votes
With your notes

A grant full of notes

As you'll ever ask for votes.
You must be DUP'd

Look Round and See the Carnage of This Scene

Inspired by: *Look Down*

Enter TORINES

TORINES

Look round and see
The carnage of this scene.
Look round, and ask
If we can make a plan.
We ask, whose fault,
It must be Theryline.
Look round, look round,
She'll do it if she can.

Enter DUPINES who join ARLINE

How do you do, We're DUP

Inspired by: *How Do You Do, My Name's Gavroche*

DUPINES

How do you do? We're DUP.
But you will need a pile of notes.
If you're still keen to leave EC,
One billion pounds will buy our votes.

We all enjoy superiority.
But the arithmetic is neat.
And you'll need us for your majority.
We know at home we're the elite.
If you're beat, if they scoff,
Buy us off! Buy us off!

How Do You Solve a Problem Like Our Brexit?

Inspired by: *How Do You Solve a Problem Like Maria?*

Enter some VOTERS, who gaze with puzzlement at THERYLINE and GOVERT

SOME VOTERS
She says that Brexit equals Brexit -
Makes no sense to me.
She holds elections, doesn't win,
And bribes the DUP.
And underneath her Brexit
All the weaknesses she'll see.
I know why Cam'rine's singing on his exit.

We're losing ways to work as one.
They want us to get real.
We're always late for everything.
We're heading for "No Deal".
I hate to have to say it,
But I very firmly feel,
That Brexit's not an asset to our country.

GOVERT:
"I'd like to say a word on his behalf".

THERYLINE:
"Then say it, Chancellor of the Duchy of Lancaster"

GOVERT
"Well, Boris makes me laugh".
All titter, including VALBORIS.

VOTERS:
How do you solve a problem like our Brexit?

How is it we have made this mess unique?
How do you solve a problem like our Brexit?
And save 350 million per week?

Many a thing the twenty-seven tell us,
And we think they think we think they are fools
But how is it we can stay,
When this is what we will say:
"We'd like to leave the club and change the rules."
Oh, how do you solve a problem like our Brexit?
How do you hold a pipedream in your hand?

Now on Brexit I'm confused,
Out of focus and bemused,
Things are never quite exactly as they seem.
And she'll say to her guys "Go, deal"
And start hoarding for a "No Deal",
It's a drama! It's a nightmare! It's a dream!
We'll increase our Customs fees,
Drive the City overseas,
It will throw the Irish border in a mess,
And the lorries that we sent
Will be parked all over Kent,
It's a headache! Now ValBoris!
Let's confess!

How do you solve a problem like our Brexit?
How do you find a plan and pin it down?
How do you get some answers on the Brexit?
From a fantasist! A Govert-wisp! A clown!
Deals with others will be taking longer,
Trade with Europe we will not enhance,
But here's what we'll achieve,

If we choose to Leave -
Our passports will be blue! (though made in France).
Oh, how do you solve a problem like our Brexit?
How do you hold a pipedream in your hand?
Exit VOTERS.

Look Round and Ask if She Can Make a Plan

Inspired by: *Look Down*

Enter TORINES and THERYLINE

TORINES
Look round, and ask if she can make a plan.
Look round, look round, she'll do it if she can.

TORINES
We are the Leaders of this land.
We are the ones who run the show.
But only one – that's Theryline -
Can make the legislation go.

THERYLINE
I am still here, not fading out.
"Won't last the week?" Well I will try.
There is some anger on your part.
I'll fix a Confidence / Supply,
Before we cut that Corboche down to size.
Before strong, stable ones arise.

Labour People

Inspired by: *Little People*

Enter CORBOCHE and LABOUR SUPPORTERS

CORBOCHE

They laugh at me because
I don't have number 10 keys.
They laugh at me because
Of low support by MPs.
I tell them I have lots of support on the ground.
The world is big,
But Labour people
Turn it around.

The Many make a sound.
The Few Gang are in charge.
But many pennies make a pound
In all we're large.
Your Deal is wrong in one sense,
Unless you talk to us.
Your promises are nonsense
Though you wrote on a bus.

Workers' Rights are crucial
If we leave the EU.
Jobs must be protected
And economy too.
I've read the EU Charter,
And I know that it's true.
A Customs Union saves the fuss,
So, let's get one through.

LABOUR SUPPORTERS
The Many must be heard.
The Few Gang are in charge.
But many pennies make a pound
In all we're large.
We will oppose your deal
Unless you talk to us.
Your promises are nonsense
Though you wrote on a bus.

LABOUR SUPPORTERS
So, listen Theryline now
With your head up the arse
Of Northern Irish Unionists
You ain't got no class.
So, keep your duff arrangements
You don't need to explain.
We'll vote you out whenever
We can end your brief reign.

Be careful as you go
For little people grow,

CORBOCHE
And Labour people know
When Labour people fight
You thought we're easy pickings,
But you found we bite.
So, don't get all grandiose,
And do not start to grouse.
You're better to behave
As if you don't own the House.
And we'll fight your legislation

And we won't give up!

LABOUR SUPPORTERS
The Many must be heard.
The Few Gang are in charge.
But many pennies make a pound,
In all we're large.
We will oppose your deal
Unless you talk to us.
Your promises are nonsense
Though you wrote on a bus.

Your promises are rubbish
Though you wrote it on a bus.
Exit all.

One's Mascot

Inspired by: *Valjean Arrested & Forgiven*

Enter THE QUEEN, *with* THERYLINE, VALBORIS, GOVERT, LAUNDRETTE, ARLINE & CORBOCHE

THE QUEEN
Well you've buffered up One's Ascot,
One does not think much of that.
One attends but wears One's mascot,
(She takes an EU beanie hat from a salver, or her pocket, and puts it on)
Blue and yellow EU hat.

When you first came to the palace,
Thinking you knew what to do,
And you sought the poisoned chalice,
Did you know you had no clue?

Well One isn't now so youthful
But do not think One is fooled
Can Prime Ministers be truthful?
As by royalty you're ruled.

You have buffered up your Party,
With a billion as a bung.
One's response, sincere and hearty -
Do not think of blaming One.

But remember this now, madam:
Show respect please for your Queen.
All your chances, have you had 'em?
One Remains when you have been.

Now see fewer friendly faces,
Your majority's gone too.
Well One's off now to the races
And the rest One leaves to you.

Exit all.

Leave and Remain – Led By Donkeys

Inspired by: *Red and Black*

Enter *WILLEAU, JAMESONNE, BENNI & OLLYVERT*

There are crowds of PEOPLE in the background.

WILLEAU

Stoke Newington the billboards are prepared.
Hackney North, The Davis Upside's up.
Students, workers, everyone
They are seeing what we've done.
With the spreading of the quotes
Everyone's tweeting notes.

JAMESONNE

The time is here.
So near it's winning the Twittersphere.
And yet beware -
Don't let the boards go to your heads.
The establishment is a dangerous foe.
They may arrest us for criminal mess.
But starting from here there's a long way to go.
If we're accused then we'll have to confess.
We need a fund – to rally the people,
To show them they're wise,
And to show them the lies.

BENNI

Ollyvert, what's up with you today?
It sounds as if you've had a thought
Let's Skype and see what's going on.

OLLYVERT

A thought you say? A thought maybe.

A crowdfund site would set us free.
One minute live – and we'd be off!

JAMESONNE
I am agog! But can we stay
Anonymous just as today?
We kept it quiet just who we are.

OLLYVERT
We talk of needing all to hide.
With funding we'll go nationwide.
We better choose to set the bar.

JAMESONNE
It is time for us all
To decide to go wild.
Do we fight for the right
To a night with a paste bucket now?
Have you asked of yourselves
What's the price they may pay?
It's not simply a game
For four Remainers to play.
The colour of these boards
Is changing day by day.

THE PEOPLE
Remain - for this they paste today.
OTHER PEOPLE
Leave – you lost, we told you so.
THE PEOPLE
Remain - we hope that we will stay.
OTHER PEOPLE
Leave – they promised we will go.

OLLYVERT
If you look at the fund
Then let's see, as we chose
That for the launch we start
With a target of ten thousand pounds.

WILLEAU
If you look at the fund
Then let's see how it goes.
How the folk may between them
Give thousands of pounds.
And what was passed seems wrong,
And what was lost seems right.

THE PEOPLE
Remain - for this they paste today.
OTHER PEOPLE
Leave – you lost, we told you so.
THE PEOPLE
Remain - the hope that we will stay.
OTHER PEOPLE
Leave – they promised we will go.

BENNI
My friends it's no longer just us.
We started small but now have funds.
On billboards we can show their flaws.

JAMESONNE
As to an unknown fate we're whirled,
We strive towards a truthful world.
And now we have an urgent cause.

THE PEOPLE
Remain - for this we paste today.
OTHER PEOPLE
Leave – you lost, we told you so.
THE PEOPLE
Remain - the hope that we will stay.
OTHER PEOPLE
Leave – they promised we will go.
All exit.

Do You See the People March?

Inspired by: *Do You Hear the People Sing?*

Enter SOME PEOPLE *with placards, marching, led by* GRIEVOUS

SOME PEOPLE

Do you see the people march?
People who want to use a pen.
It is the marching of a people
Who will not be fooled again.
When campaigning from both sides
Sticks to remaining in the truth,
There is a chance, to make a choice,
In the polling booth.

We will live again in freedom
In the countries of UK
And determine final outcome
And we'll have the Final Say
The lies will be busted
And truth will prevail on that day.

Do you see the people march?
People who want to use a pen.
It is the marching of a people
Who will not be fooled again.
When campaigning from both sides
Sticks to remaining in the truth,
There is a chance, to make a choice,
In the polling booth.

(REPEAT from "We will live again in freedom" *then all exit).*

Sturgene Comes Too?

Inspired by: *Plumet Attack*

Enter THERYLINE, GOVERT *and* VALBORIS *and* LAUNDRETTE

THERYLINE

This is the plan.
I've worked out all my red lines.
I'll keep myself to myself;
They'll give in! Watch for the signs.
I smell vict'ry here.

Two years ago
We met and had a big vote
Which is my destiny
To fulfil, don't mind if I gloat.

GOVERT
What do I care
Which folk will sob?
Vict'ry I'll share
Finish the job!

Enter STURGENE, *initially unseen by* THERYLINE.

THERYLINE
Ireland and all
We will be out.
Sturgene comes too.
Just have no doubt.

LAUNDRETTE
Look who's here, it's Sturgene.
She heard you say her name.
Why's she bothering us now?

THERYLINE
Sturgene, now get on home.
You're not needed in this.
We're enough here without you.

STURGENE
I know your game.
I tell you we don't like what you played.
You are going from the EU.
We want ordinary trade.

THERYLINE
Don't interfere;
In the same boat.
You must stay here.
You had a vote.

GOVERT
She's going soft.
We're going hard.
Go home, Sturgene.
Go home, this is our way.

STURGENE
I'm going to scream! Going to warn my folk here!

THERYLINE
If you will scream you will regret it

For a year.

VALBORIS
What a palaver!
What an absolute farce!
Let's agree to throw Sturgene
Out on her arse!

GOVERT
Not a sound out of you!

STURGENE
Well I said that I'd call it.
Said that I'd call it.
*(STURGENE Screams **"INDY REFERENDUM"**)*

CORBOCHE runs on looking startled.

THERYLINE
Head off to Chequers! Don't hang around.
Leave her to me! She is unsound!
You wait Sturgene. That is not right.
You'll get no votes. You'll see the light.
ALL EXIT except THERYLINE, CORBOCHE and STURGENE.

CORBOCHE
It was your cry as I did note,
They will tell you, in the same boat.
Well now Sturgene, asking for this,
I am not keen, but you have your vote!
EXIT THERYLINE, following GOVERT & co.
EXIT STURGENE and CORBOCHE in conversation.

One Day More at Chequers

Inspired by: *One Day More*

Enter THERYLINE, GOVERT, LAUNDRETTE, VALBORIS and DAVIDE DAVINE.

In this song, all wander around the stage, but THERYLINE is always on her own, VALBORIS and DAVIDE DAVINE are conspiratorial together, and GOVERT observes them from a distance, but with occasional comment.

THERYLINE
One day more!
Another plan, another Chequers farce.
At least I told them if they want their cars,
These folks I put in Cabinet
Cannot resign or not just yet -
One day more!

VALBORIS
I did not drive myself today.
How to get back if resignation?

GOVERT
One day more.

DAVIDE DAVINE
Tomorrow I'll be off to play.
I've had enough negotiation.

THERYLINE
One more day to bang the heads.

VALBORIS
Will we ever meet again?

DAVIDE DAVINE
One more day of pointless wonder.

VALBORIS
I don't want to be with you.

DAVIDE DAVINE
What a job I might have done!

VALBORIS
Will you wait until we're done
I'm fed up, Let's leave EU

DAVIDE DAVINE
One more day till I resign!.........................

VALBORIS
Do I follow when he goes?

DAVIDE DAVINE
To the benches of our freedom!

VALBORIS
Shall I join old Davide there?

DAVIDE DAVINE
You can come but please don't whine!

VALBORIS
Do I go, so do I dare?

DAVIDE DAVINE
Don't go today, you'll lose your car.

VALBORIS
It is too far
To lose your car!

DAVIDE DAVINE
One day more?

THERYLINE
One more day to get agreement.
By tonight, sign up they should.
Then I'll know that they support me,
In the House, they will be good

Enter FARAGIER to one side. He stays well away from the others but comments on what he sees, as follows:

FARAGIER
She can ban a dither
She can hold them all.
Doesn't mean they're with her,
For the curtain call,
Here a little doubt
There a little slow;
Doesn't mean we're out
The way she thinks we'll go.

VALBORIS
One day to a new existence.

DAVIDE DAVINE
Get the contracts for the jobs.

DAVIDE DAVINE
We'll express our resistance.

VALBORIS & DAVIDE DAVINE
We'll express our resistance.

VALBORIS
There are jobs with Telegraph.

DAVIDE DAVINE
Better dosh than Foreign Sec job.

VALBORIS
Do you hear my hollow laugh?
My place is there!
I'll leave with you!

DAVIDE DAVINE
One day more!

FARAGIER
Watch the buggers run
Don't know what they need
This is so much fun
It's such a mess indeed.
She can think it's done.
And it's all agreed.
She won't get agreement
And she will be pee'd.
(He laughs)

VALBORIS & DAVIDE DAVINE
It's been a drag until today,
So many briefs and bits of paper

THERYLINE
I'll reserve their lanky gofers.
They won't go – they'd lose their cars,
And as well their swanky chauffeurs.
Any doubts, out on their arse.

DAVIDE DAVINE
One more day to have this farce.

VALBORIS
One day more.

VALBORIS & DAVIDE DAVINE
Tomorrow -s resignation day.
But just today we'll say we're staying.

VALBORIS
One more day to resignation.
When I'm home I'll dump the car.
I'll regret this assignation.

VALBORIS & DAVIDE DAVINE
Tomorrow we'll be far away.
Tomorrow's resignation day.
DAVIDE and VALBORIS exit arm in arm as they sing this.

ALL
Tomorrow we'll discover.

What the Chequers headlines have in store.
One more night! One more day! One day more!

Exit GOVERT and LAUNDRETTE.
Only THERYLINE is left on stage. (We nearly said "Remains on stage"!)

Then a big letter arrives for THERYLINE (dropped from above)
She picks it up to read it.
As she does so another letter arrives.

THERYLINE *(quietly, recalling)*
"Tomorrow we'll discover.
What the Chequers headlines have in store.
One more night! One more day! One day more!"

On My Own

Inspired by: *On My Own*

THERYLINE
And now I'm all alone again,
They both resigned,
They've given up now
They think it's wrecked,
And what comes next,
They think that I will muck it up now.

And now the end is near.
Now I can make believe we're clear.
I tried another Dominic to give the words a going over,
But seemingly he didn't know the way to Calais out of Dover.
I'm trying not to laugh,
But you just cannot get the staff.

On my own -
As now they're not beside me.
I'm alone,
Cos Boris did deride me.

Without him
His thinks that I did wrongly.
So, have I lost my way? Oh no,
I'm stable very strongly.

With EU, negotiation follows.
Though there's some that think that we can never
Achieve it, but Brussels has its summits.
And all I see's withdrawal forever and forever.

And I know, that Ireland is a fudge.

But the backstop means the can kicked down the road.
When I go, though Tories may not budge.
Still I say, that border be blowed.

I love it, each page that we have writ.
I love it, though others think it's shit.

Without it
My premiership is pointless,
For Brexit equals Brexit though
I may not have supporters.

I love it,
But each debate I'm learning,
Through my reign,
The time is not extending.

Without it
We would be still Remaining,
For Brexit equals Brexit though
There's no-one was complaining.

I love it
I love it
I love it
So stably on my own.

An Agreement Running to 585 Pages

Inspired by: *Stars*

THERYLINE:
There, out of the chaos
An agreement running
To five eight five pages -
Five eight five pages.
Please be my witness
I never shall yield
Till it pass all the stages,
Till it pass all the stages.

I signed it off just last night.
Mine is the way of the light.
Those who follow the path of the government -
I'll tell them they're right.
And if they go,
Like Boris and co,
Well well,
They might.

MPs, in your multitudes,
Soon to be counted,
Filling the Commons,
With Tories and might,
You are my followers,
Stable and strong,
Keeping Bills to the Right,
Keeping Bills to the Right.

You know your place as my serfs.
You hold your course and your wills,
And each in election

Returns and returns,
You know all of our Bills,
And if you fall
Like Boris and co,
You fall,
No frills.

And so, we have pages, and so they are written,
With chapters, headings and footnotes,
And we will follow,
And we will call,
Meaningful Votes.

You're to be counted,
Ending the chaos,
With order and light,
You are my followers,
Stable and strong.
Keeping Bills to the Right.

You as Prime Minster Listen to This

Inspired by: *The Attack*

Enter VALBORIS, GOVERT, LAUNDRETTE, REES-MOGGI &TORINES

REES-MOGGI
You as Prime Minster listen to this,
No one is coming to help you to vote.
You're on your own.
Give up your Deal and go.

THERYLINE
Damn their warnings, Damn their notes.
They will see the Tories' votes.

She attempts to conduct VALBORIS, GOVERT, LAUNDRETTE, REES-MOGGI &TORINES to echo this song, and to stand with her, but VALBORIS, REES-MOGGI &TORINES leave her with GOVERT and LAUNDRETTE on one side of the stage and move together to the other side, singing:

VALBORIS, REES-MOGGI &TORINES
Cram the lobbies, Slam the notes.
She will see the Tories' votes.

A Little Vote of Pain

Inspired by: *A Little Fall of Rain*

THERYLINE is still standing. VALBORIS is by her side. The other politicians observe from a distance.

THERYLINE
Don't you fret, oh ValBoris,
I think I'm still alive.
Defeat by Two three five
Is not the final word.
There's hope. A little braidie bird
Will help to get a vote
Will help keep me afloat.
It passed! – with backstop gone, you heard?

VALBORIS
You think you'll live Ther'line, I think I'll shove,
As you are in the job which still I'd love.

THERYLINE
Just hold the vote, so legally,
With different words, and let us see.

VALBORIS
You won't live a hundred days,
And I will show you how
I will desert you now.

THERYLINE
The vote can't hurt me now.
The vote will now replace what's past
And you can sack me when,
And you can sack me then.
(VALBORIS comes to her side and embraces her).

I'll go now, I'm resigned at last.
The vote that brings you in is double cursed.
I said that I would go, so do your worst.
Still votes away from winning this,
And I'll not have that bliss.

GOVERT, DAVIDE DAVINE, REES-MOGG and TORINES enter silently and reverently surrounding THERYLINE'S death-couch.

THERYLINE
So, don't you fret, oh Valboris.
I think that you will find,
It's time that I resigned,
(collapses onto a couch)
And you'll be leader then,

That's all I need to know.
You'll take the poisoned cup,
And you will stuff it up.
And votes
Will make the Tories …*(sighs)*

VALBORIS *(interrupting)*
Hushabye, dear Theryline.
This ending is quite neat.
Now think of
Fields of wheat.
You'll run
so light and free.
I'm here,

I'll stay in play.
Till resignation
And votes -
The votes will be for ….
….me!

THERYLINE dies, but her soul rises from her death-bed and she runs off into (projected) fields of wheat.
OR – the other people on the stage represent the fields of wheat, and as she runs off, they sway to let her through.

Exit all, excitedly talking

Brexit's A Musical Trick – Act 3 (Boris ValBoris)

Bring Him In

Inspired by: *Bring Him Home*

Enter REES-MOGGI, LAUNDREETE, GOVERT and GAVINI who carry a mute VALBORIS around the stage.

GAVINI
Tories all,
Hear the call,
In our need
We can count on you all.
He is blond. It's a stunt
Let him win. He won't hunt.

Bring him in
Bring him in
Vote him in.
He's like a demon full of sin
If we had looked for such a one
Our summers since referendum
How soon they fly, how quick they come.
With Russian gold,
He will be dumb.
Bring him votes;
Let him rule.
He is blond. He is only a fool.

You can vote. You can choose.
Let him win. He will booze.

If he wins, we will win.
Let him win, Bring him in.
Bring him in.
Bring him in.
They sit the silent VALBORIS down on a chair

Vote for Him, for Days Gone By

Inspired by: *Drink with Me*

REES-MOGGI
Vote for him, for days gone by.
Lent some votes, saw Govert out
Here's to pretty girl,
If truth you will ferret.
That's a witty girl,
With cash earned on merit.
Here's to her.
And here's my shout.

TORINES join in
Vote for him, for days gone by,
For the world that used to be.
For our fine smart tax takes
Never say die.
May our line of tax breaks
Never run dry.

Enter CUNNINGS, who directs the TORINES to sit down
CUNNINGS
Now he's through
So comfortably.

REES-MOGGI
Do I care about this job?
Now Theryline, had time, to flee.
And we don't need her,
Take a turn at the wheel,
I'll be House Leader,
And we'll pass a new Deal.
I'll explain, to you, about Me.

Through the next song, all except REES-MOGGI look on with a touch of bewilderment, except BORIS VALBORIS who stirs in his chair and looks on approvingly.

I am the Very Model of a Prejudiced Etonian

Inspired by: *I am the Very Model of a Modern Major-General*

I am the very model of a prejudiced Etonian.
My diction is impeccable, my politics draconian,
I'm quite the polar opposite of what you'd call revisionist,
And though I went to public school, at least I'm not a
Wykehamist.
I'm keeping the tradition of the gentry ent'ring politics,
How else are we to keep away the Corbynista Bolsheviks?
So through my vivid promises of dividends most decorous,
I've mobilised the Brexiteers to levels quite obstreperous,
I whip them up to frenzy in a manner so Pavlovian.
They do not seem to see that it's increasingly dystopian,
So here I stand before you like a skeletal Napoleon,
I am the very model of a prejudiced Etonian.

I've studied all the Classics from Herodotus to Sophocles.
How else am I to criticise my colleagues' etymologies?
Perhaps that's why I vote against most freedoms and equalities.
These authors are about as old as most of my philosophies!
I know of all the backwards Parliament'ry curiosities.
Like letting Commons' priv'lege keep me safe to spout atrocities.
I know the terminologies, chronologies and glossaries.
And yet I still behave as if we never lost the colonies.
I often drain the public funds to renovate my properties,
Although I have more money than some smaller world economies.
I never make apologies for lack of reciprocities,
Despite the fact that swathes of Britons lack basic commodities!

My views on social issues haven't changed much since the Tudor
times.
I rage against the slightest change to long-outdated paradigms.
I lack the base ability to sympathise or empathise.
My Commons' sprawl exemplifies the privilege I symbolise.
When criticised on Women's Rights I hide behind Catholicism,
Bending it to justify my heart-of-stone Conservatism,
Yet I sound the clarion of fear of fundamentalism.
Without seeming to acknowledge this inherent dualism,
I try to paint a picture of a Brexit most utopian,
And when they all explain to me the likely pandemonium,
I patronise my critics with my methods Ciceronian,
I am the very model of a prejudiced Etonian.

By Robin Wallington

Help Us Out

Inspired by: *Come to Me*

Enter FARAGIER and TORINE BACKERS who join VALBORIS, CUNNINGS and the others. Some of the BACKERS have Russian hats and Russian accents

BACKERS
Boris, it's turned so tough.
Boris, we fear for tax avoidance.
We've played the markets all,
But fear new regulation.

Help us out, for we are earning stacks.
Boris, please, we need to pay no tax,
Help us out, we don't want regulation.
We badly need to keep our breaks not stay an EU nation.

Let's get out, we must retain our plenty.
Get us out, before it's twenty twenty.
There's a dark threat, which mandates more transparency,
And threatens everything we do in every modern currency.

VALBORIS
O my friends, our time is running out.
But my friends, I swear I'll do or die.

BACKERS
Please Boris, where all the markets play.

VALBORIS
Have a peace, have a piece today.

BACKERS
Our tax breaks

VALBORIS & CUNNINGS
They still will have protection.

BACKERS
Our tax breaks

VALBORIS & CUNNINGS
We will be out by Autumn.

BACKERS
Oh Boris, we'd like to give you thousands,

VALBORIS & CUNNINGS
And none shall take away your breaks
If we escape the checking.

BACKERS
Make us safe.
We need these rules avoided.

VALBORIS
Well I will keep you safe.

BACKERS
We'll trust you
So we can go on playing.

VALBORIS & CUNNINGS
You need pay no tax.

BACKERS
Yes indeed, and that is what we're saying.
And so, Boris, we love you,
And we'll fund you what you need.
All exit except VALBORIS and GOVERT

I Dreamed a Dream.

Inspired by: *I Dreamed a Dream*

Enter CAMERINE with his book. He goes Centre Stage.
GOVERT joins VALBORIS to watch from the sides

CAMERINE
There was a time Govert was kind,
Boris' thinking was strong.
And they weren't complaining.
There was a time we weren't behind,
And they'd play along,
And they backed Remaining
There was a time
Then it all went wrong.

I dreamed a dream in times gone by,
When hope was high for referendum.
I dreamed, that Tory doubts would die,
As with the vote, at last we'd end 'em.
Then I was young, it's true to tell.
Speeches were made, who'll be my backer?
Fed up with pretty Patel,
But still I feared I couldn't sack her.

Enter CUNNINGS
With the Cunnings of the night,
And Govert said

GOVERT
"No more experts."

CAMERINE
With their warnings by the Right,

Were they winning with their race?
We slept that summer, were not wise;
"Be filled with a million guest Turks?"

GOVERT VALBORIS and CUNNINGS are highly amused by this, dig each other in the ribs etc

They sent the adverts with the lies,
Which then were gone from Book of Face.

And still I dream of the EC;
A second vote, perhaps, I feel.
But there are dreams that cannot be,
As Tories drive towards a Deal.
I had a dream the vote would be,
So different from that hell of lying,
So different from these Brexit memes
And now they've killed the dream
I dreamed.

Exit CAMERINE, shaking his head sorrowfully.

Here's Some Russian Gold

Inspired by: *Dog Eats Dog*

Enter VALBORIS and CUNNINGS with some BACKERS

VALBORIS
Here's some Russian gold
From our Russian friends.
Pardon me, comrade,
Very generous of you I'm sure.
Shouldn't be too hard to hide.
Add them to our list.
But keep their names quiet.
Here, among the dodgy bits,
Let us enjoy the ride.
For stuff like this we lied.

CUNNINGS
Here's a happy gift,
That will spirits lift.
Wouldn't want to show it;
That would really blow their minds.
Thanks comrade, I'm in your debt.

Enter GRIEVOUS with a report for VALBORIS to sign.
VALBORIS refuses.

VALBORIS
Here's a little bung,
If you hold your tongue.
Report we will defer it,
Of the Russian interference.
That report's a ticking bomb.

CUNNINGS
Well someone got to make short deals my friends.
Before the No Deal harvest
Passes by and we can stash.
Someone's got to clean up before this all ends.
When the UK leaves and CRASH.

VALBORIS
It's a world where the bears eat the bears.
Where they want to spread hunger and tears.
And reports from the peers,
That might raise some fears
Will be dead to the world till the vote.
I hold my pen and don't sign it off,
And no-one can stop me now.
So, no-one stops me now.

Exit all except GRIEVOUS

Empty Houses, Empty Benches

Inspired by: *Empty Chairs at Empty Tables*

GRIEVOUS
In my humble speech I've spoken
Of behaviour that we've seen.
For our Parliament is broken
And he told lies to the Queen.

Here he talked of prorogation,
And he chose a 5-week slot.
Manly idleness oration?
He disparaged "Girly Swot".

From the pen of that adviser
They could see a House unplugged.
And they went with Privy Council,
And I can hear them now.
The very lies that they had said
Become their own conviction.
As they planned the Houses both prorogued,

Oh, my friends, my friends, don't let them.
If we're gone then they will play -
Empty Houses, empty benches,
We should not be sent away.

Scrutiny for legislation
Missed its chance if we're not here.
Empty Houses, empty benches -
Making MPs disappear.

Oh, my friends, my friends, don't ask me.
What the heck this plan was for -
Empty Houses, empty benches,
And there's scrutiny no more.

There Was a Wise Lady Who Tackled a Lie

Inspired by: *There Was an Old Lady Who Swallowed a Fly*

Enter PANNINI and CHORUS. GRIEVOUS looks on.

Enter SUPREME JUDGE who takes her seat in Court.

PANNINI:
There was a wise lady who tackled a lie -
A lie to the Queen with never a sigh.
CHORUS
The lie will die.

PANNINI:
There was a wise lady who sported a spider,
They wriggled and squiggled and tried to misguide her.
CHORUS:
She sported the spider to catch the lie.
A lie to the Queen with never a sigh.
The lie will die.

PANNINI:
There was a wise lady was undeterred.
Quite undeterred by what she heard.
CHORUS:
She's undeterred to wear a spider.
They wriggled and squiggled and tried to misguide her.
She sported the spider to catch the lie.
A lie to the Queen with never a sigh.
The lie will die.

PANNINI:
There was a wise lady who squashed them flat.
Fancy that, with all who sat.
CHORUS:
She squashed them flat, quite undeterred.

Quite undeterred, to wear a spider?
They wriggled and squiggled and tried to misguide her.
She sported the spider to catch the lie.
A lie to the Queen with never a sigh.
The lie will die.

PANNINI:
There was a wise lady who cleared the fog.
One lower court was stuck in a bog.
CHORUS:
She cleared the fog to squash them flat.
She squashed them flat, quite undeterred.
Quite undeterred, to wear a spider?
They wriggled and squiggled and tried to misguide her.
She sported the spider to catch the lie.
A lie to the Queen with never a sigh.
The lie will die.

PANNINI:
There was a wise lady who took full note
Of scrutiny needs and time to vote.
CHORUS:
She took full note to clear the fog.
She cleared the fog to squash them flat.
She squashed them flat, quite undeterred.
Quite undeterred, to wear a spider?
They wriggled and squiggled and tried to misguide her.
She sported the spider to catch the lie.
A lie to the Queen with never a sigh.
The lie will die.

PANNINI:
There was a wise lady who worked out how
To get Parliament back and working now.
CHORUS:
She worked out how and took full note.
She took full note to clear the fog.
She cleared the fog to squash them flat.
She squashed them flat, quite undeterred.
Quite undeterred, to wear a spider?
They wriggled and squiggled and tried to misguide her.
She sported the spider to catch the lie.
A lie to the Queen with never a sigh.
The lie will die.

PANNINI:
There was a wise lady who heard their thoughts.
She's Queen of Courts.
Exit all

Voting, Voting

Inspired by: *Turning*

Enter VOTERS

VOTERS

Did you see them? Heck they are a shower.
Russian interference, and they're hanging on to power.
Further, further
To the right they veer.
Never will they open up
A report that they all fear,
Postpone publish till some time next year.

Who will stop them? Only voters do.
Look at all the lies they tell,
And then try to see through.
Are they fearful?
Why tell all these lies?
If you see the truth they hide
They'll be cut down to size.
Out of falsehoods let the truth arise

Nasty changes? This will not be fun.
Now it sounds like punishment to "Let's get Brexit done".
Don't be fooled now. That won't be the end.
Unless we are voting now a clear sign to send
Voting, voting, voting, voting, voting
For this to end.

Voting, voting, voting, this to end
Voting that is tactical the right MPs to send
Else nowt changes, nothing ever can.
Round and round the carousel, and back where you began.
Round and round and back where you began.
Exit all

Soliloquy – Caught by Benn

Inspired by: *Soliloquy*

Enter VALBORIS

VALBORIS:

Who is this man?
What sort of devil is he?
To have me caught by the Benn,
And then not let me go free?
It was the hour I thought
When I would triumph for real.
And now I am caught.
He thinks I can't go No Deal.
All it would take was a flick of the pen
To leave at Halloween,
But now I'm handicapped by Benn!

Damned if I'll live with those rebels of mine.
Damned if I'll let them remain on this ship.
I am PM and PM is not mocked.
I'll see rebellion, and withdraw the Whip.
There is no way that I'll have appeal.
It is either my way or No Deal.

How can I now allow these folks
To take the Order Paper on.
These desp'rate folks that I have clashed with.
They gave me nought. They check my freedom.

They must be banished by my hand.
That is what's right.
And it is best to do tonight.
So, twenty-one get out of sight!

But was that quite so cute?
Was it my smartest wheeze?
Shall their sins be forgiven?
And I've lost those MPs!

And must I now fight on without
The votes of twenty-one Tories.
Cunnings was clear I had to do it.
The lead I once had is lost and broken.
Is Cunnings wise or is he dumb?
And does he know
In sending out the twenty-one
He may have killed us even so?

I am stumbling and I fall,
And the lobbies make me frown,
As I stare into the news
Of minority let-down.
Amber Rudder's gone as well
And my Government is weak
Was this Heaven? It is Hell !
And I don't know how to speak……..

Ain't It a Laugh

Inspired by: *Beggar at the Feast*

Enter CUNNINGS with GOVERT and REES-MOGGI.

CUNNINGS
Ain't it a laugh? Hey this is real.
You missed your chance to do a Deal.

VALBORIS
Look at you all.
Hey big girl's blouse.
You had a Bill
We sent to the House.
Europe in my sights.
Putty in my hand.
And here's me making up
Ways to fix Ireland.

Merkel said "A month",
I said "Thank you Ma'am".
There's a goodly time
To do a bit of harm.
Anything at all
That we'll say we've done
Give away the backstop,
And we'll say we've won.

VALBORIS & CUNNINGS
Taking a new Deal to London,
And we hope MPs fed up.

VALBORIS & GOVERT.
We're the ones who'll make it.
We're the ones who'll fake it all sped up.

VALBORIS & CUNNINGS
Watch the voters cringe.
Watch the worried looks.
Keep your wits about you.
As we cook the books.
Masters of the work.
Masters of the scare.
Clear away the Workers' Rights.
We'll get our share.

We like fixing legislation.
Money is the stuff we smell.

VALBORIS.
And when I've made my fortune,
You can auction off the rest to Hell!

It is Passed

Inspired by: *You Will Live*

VALBORIS
Now you are here.
You're all beside me.
Now we can vote in peace
And have the Second Reading.

GOVERT
It is passed! Boris your Deal is passed.
But it's too soon, to think that that is all.

VALBORIS
And so Govert, support me now to lie.
I'll dissolve, I will try.

On this vote,
I call the dissolution.
Mark this well.
It is final solution.
It's a story
Of lies and misbehaviour.
I have ignored requirements
Of British constitution.

VALBORIS appears weak with frustration

Enter the GHOSTS OF THERYLINE & CAMERINE. They address the weakened VALBORIS.

THERYLINE & CAMERINE
Come with us
To place of lost Prime Ministers.
On your bus,
At last, at last not sinister.

Write your memoirs;
It's time to leave your vows and
You'll make a pretty penny.

VALBORIS *(dreamily)*
I could give talks for thousands

VALBORIS *(becoming energised again)*
No! My Deal *(picks up Withdrawal Agreement)*
Of clauses a selection.
(To GOVERT and REES-MOGGI)
Take my hand
And lead me to election.
There's arrangements
That work so manfully;
There won't be customs checks performed
Upon the Irish Sea.

Bridge Over Doubled Borders

Inspired by: *Bridge over Troubled Waters*

VALBORIS
When you're bleary, caught by Benn,
When all are asking you, "Hey Boris, when?"
I'm on my side, oh, when bets get short,
And friends are on the pound,
Like a bridge over doubled borders,
I will play around.
Like a bridge over doubled borders,
I will play around.

When you're down and out,
When you're on the dole,
When meals are hard to find.
I won't comfort you
Not take your part, oh, when No-Deal comes.
And men won't give a pound.
Like a bridge over doubled borders
I will play around.
Like a bridge over doubled borders
I will play around.

Fail on Raab Govert.
Fail on by.
Your plans have come to shine.
All your ads are on their way.
We don't need wine.
Oh, Halloween's the end.
I'm bluffing right behind.
Like a bridge over doubled borders
I have lost my mind.
Like a bridge over doubled borders.

I have lost my mind.

I'm sorry that I lied.
To the Queen.
My time may come to end;
All my dreams are on the way.
My book, my talks.
"Oh, if you'd let me Brexit."
I'll make my fortune, fine.
Like a bridge over doubled borders,
I have lost my mind.
Like a bridge over doubled borders.
I have lost my mind.

All move to one side of the Stage.
Enter the rest of the cast, except THE PEOPLE *and* GRIEVOUS *who enter for the final song,*

Do You See the People March?

Inspired by: *Do You Hear the People Sing?*

Enter THE PEOPLE and GRIEVOUS

PEOPLE

Do you see the people march?
People who want to use a pen.
It is the marching of a people
Who will not be fooled again.
When campaigning from both sides
Sticks to remaining in the truth,
There is a chance, to make a choice,
In the polling booth.

They will live again in freedom
In the countries of UK
They will determine final outcome
They will have the Final Say
The lies will be busted
And truth will prevail on that day

GRIEVOUS *(to audience):*

Do you hear what's happened here?
Are you concerned when people cheat?
Have you concluded on the evidence,
That #BrexitsATrickNotATreat?
Do you recall how this played out?
Are you now with Brexit bored?
#BrexitsAMusicalTrick,
As we have just explored.

What the hell was yet to happen,
Since our scribe put down his pen?
What ridiculous events occur,

With who and what and when?
We're surely not likely to tackle this shitshow again?

Do you hear what's happened here?
Are you concerned when people cheat?
Have you concluded on the evidence,
That #BrexitsATrickNotATreat?
Do you recall how this played out?
Are you now with Brexit bored?
#BrexitsAMusicalTrick,
As we have just explored.

Failure Doesn't Matter in the Past

Inspired by: *Beggar at the Feast*

Enter CUNNINGS with VALBORIS.

CUNNINGS
Ain't it a laugh?
Now how d'you feel
Forget what I said
On having a Deal.
Ireland command
Won't be obeyed.
And so we can't
Fix that East to West trade.

VALBORIS
Virus coming close,
Countries shutting down.
But here's me in the phone box
As the Clark Kent clown

CUNNINGS
Master of the Con.
Teller of the Lie.
Yesterday is soon gone
When you blink your eye.

Both dance around the stage firing SPADs and Civil Servants

VALBORIS
Never mind the facts.
Give me your support.

Optimism to the max,

CUNNINGS
Indeed you ought.

VALBORIS
Trading we will need a system.
Should have thought of that before.

CUNNINGS
But we took our pledges.
We took them and we pissed them up the wall.

VALBORIS
Others will shut down,
That is not for us.
Superman is flying
To his big red bus.
Herd immunity,
Mostly old will die.
Meanwhile we'll pretend to Build.
I don't know why.

CUNNINGS & VALBORIS
Somehow, we'll be like Australia.
Check how well that tale will last.
Just another word for failure;
Failure doesn't matter in the past.

(Repeat from "Never Mind the Facts")

Synopsis and Notes for full Musical

Act 1 Camerine

The MP Mr Grievous introduces the musical,
"So, enjoy the presentation, which will all be done in song.
It isn't finished yet and so we hope it's not too long.
If you have opinions please tell us in case we are wrong!".
The voters bemoan austerity ("Look Round").
Boris ValBoris considers his options ("Do or Die"). ("Can I conceal the truth from everyone, And lead this gang until the vote is done?
And must the cause I did decry, Be just my cause though there's no 'why', Must I lie?")
The voters start to consider how to vote. They voice their different interests but unite their various concerns on the line "We Know What We're Voting For". Camerine and ValBoris discuss this. ("Now bring referendum twenty-sixteen on. My coalition with the Lib Dems is gone. You know what that means? Yes, it means you're free") ValBoris declares his intentions to Camerine. Voters consider whether they are in a fantasy world ("Brexitian Fantasy"). The referendum is held.
"Leave campaign from the beginning, Made some claims that were not right. But it seems the scores show winning, For the Leave team?"
"That is right. "
"But now Dave you left so early, Something surely slipped your mind? You forgot implementation. Would you leave this task behind?"
Camerine nonetheless decides to depart, warning his Party as he does so. There is a dramatic confrontation between ValBoris and Govert. ValBoris rues his wasted chance ("What Have I done?").
The Torines nonetheless need to have an election ("At the End of the Day We Have Need of a Leader") and Laundrette drops out leaving Theryline as the new leader.

Act 2 Theryline

Theryline is caught with the notes for a speech in which she spoke for Remain ("It's a hell of a speech"), but she tries to persuade Rees-Moggi and the Ergines that she is now on their side ("Well it's true that I spoke and I spoke as Remainer, But I thought at that time that the Leave team would lose. Now I've moved into the Leave gang, No-one should grieve, Please accept my excuse"). They decide to watch her carefully. Rees-Moggi explain the importance of tax evasion. ("Lovely Tax Breaks"). He wears down Theryline's resistance, but she still holds out for a transition period. She dreams about her fantasy Deal ("There is a Deal that can be done; I dream about that cherry pick; I'd like to do that deal so quick; My deal, so from EU we'll run.").

We then meet Faragier, with Widdy; he is making a song and dance about being in charge ("Master of the Spiel"). This seems to have very little to do with what else is going on,

The question arises as to whether Theryline on her own can do the Deal ("What to do"), which Lord Pannini QC opposes, and the Supreme Court determines is Parliament's responsibility.

Having secured approval, Theryline gives notice ("Knowing me, Knowing EU"), and TUSKER replies ("Go now go; and shut the door; Negotiate your trade deals, we won't do them any more"). Theryline sings about her destiny ("I Saw the Polls") and what else she needs ("Strong and Stable"). She reflects with Crosbi on what then goes wrong! ("A poll full of votes"). Arline comes to the rescue. ("How do you do? We're DUP; But you will need a pile of notes; If you're still keen to leave EC; One billion pounds will buy our votes."). Brexit is still a challenge. ("How do you solve a problem like our Brexit?").

Theryline plans to "cut that Corboche down to size", but the irrepressible Corboche bounces cheekily up. ("They laugh at me because I don't have number 10 keys. They laugh at me because of low support by MPs. I tell them I have lots of support on the ground. The world is big but Labour people turn it around").

The queen is unimpressed by Theryline's antics. ("Well you've buffered up One's Ascot, One does not think much of that. One attends but wears One's mascot, Blue and yellow EU hat").
LedByDonkeys arrive with paste buckets. ("It is time for us all to decide to go wild. Do we fight for the right To a night with a paste bucket now? Have you asked of yourselves What's the price they may pay? It's not simply a game For 4 Remainers to play. The colour of these boards Is changing day by day.").
People march and sing seeking a Final-Say. ("Do you See the People March?")
Theryline feels she has a plan with redlines, but Sturgene discovers the plan and threatens to scream "Indy referendum" if they continue, and that's what happens. Corboche admits he would not be keen but that ultimately Sturgene would get her way with him.
The Tories head off to Chequers.
In a dramatic interaction ValBoris and his pal Davide Davine consider how much longer they can stand working with Theryline ("One Day More" is their conclusion).
But Theryline's mind is on higher things and she achieves her Deal ("585-page agreement") even if ValBoris and his pal will fall.
Theryline is warned of an attack ("You as Prime Minister Listen to this").
Theryline is wounded by the attack ("A Little Vote of Pain"). ValBoris is by her side. ("You think you'll live Ther'line, I think I'll shove, As you are in the job which still I'd love.") and Theryline dies, but her soul leaves her body to run through fields of wheat.

Act 3 Boris ValBoris

Gavini and the Torines carry in a mute and apparently inactive ValBoris ("Bring him in") and sit him on a chair as their new leader. They sing "Vote For Him, for Days Gone by". Rees-Moggi reflects on this and decides "I'll explain, to you, about Me".
In a very frank discourse, he explains "I am the very Model of a Prejudiced Etonian". Rees-Moggi is joined by some Backers, some

of them Russian, and they sing ("Help us Out") to ValBoris, who promises "We will be out by Autumn".

Camerine makes a surprise return to sing a sad refrain ("I dreamed a dream", realising "But there are dreams that cannot be").

ValBoris discovers some riches in dark places ("Here's Some Russian gold").

Mr Grievous returns to bemoan that Parliament is not sitting ("Empty House and Empty Benches"). However, this question is taken to a Wise Lady by Lord Pannini QC ("There was a wise lady who tackled a lie - A lie to the Queen with never a sigh. The lie will die.")

The Voters wonder whether anything will make any difference ("Did you see them? Heck they are a shower.

Russian interference, and they're hanging on to power.")

ValBoris questions how he has been bewitched by Benn

""Who is this man; what sort of devil is he?"

We meet Cunnings however who is quite amused by events

"Ain't it a laugh? Hey this is real.

You missed your chance, To do a Deal."

Govert assures ValBoris that he will live and that his Deal is passed. But ValBoris now has thoughts of the afterlife and his books and talks. The ghosts of Theryline and Camerine invite ValBoris ("Come with us, To place of lost Prime Ministers; On your bus, At last at last not sinister").

ValBoris is tempted, but instead allows Govert and Rees-Moggi to "Take my hand, and lead me to election",

ValBoris is bleary and uncertain ("Bridge Over Doubled Borders").

The people march

("Do you see the people march, People who want to use a pen").

Events then move on towards their conclusion because "Failure Doesn't Matter in the Past " we are told by the leader and his assistant.

Brexit's A Musical Trick - The Musical - Notes

(Brexit, the Miserable Musical)

Where you recognise the original songs – and most of us do – I hope you'll enjoy reading or singing along through this blockbuster musical of the key Brexit events.

If you are more ambitious, the musical has been written to be performed, but adaptation is possible to suit the stage. Or you could arrange a concert performance where the singers sing in character, but without acting out the drama (which is easier because you don't need to learn the words).

If you are interested in staging "Brexit's A Musical Trick", or perhaps a concert performance, please get in touch via the website www.viewdelta.com. We would like to help.

Any necessary permissions for the use of performing copyrighted music are the responsibility of the organisation producing any stage show (or concert).

All appropriate thanks and apologies are due to Alain Boublil , Claude- Michel Schönberg and Herbert Kretzmer.

We should also not forget Victor Hugo from whose pen the masterpiece of "Les Misérables" with its eternal themes of justice versus love first flowed.

Our baseline for the many parody songs based on "Les Misérables" is the 1985 recording of the London stage show. The sequence tends to follow the sequence of the stage show but with a few variations. To match our story, some songs repeat, and some additional songs have been inserted; but within each song, you should find that the words contained here match the rhythm of the music exactly.

Some songs therefore may feature at times that you didn't expect them, and some lines may be sung by characters other than those you might expect, and therefore on occasion in a different octave.

So please enjoy your "Brexit's a Musical Trick" karaoke nights if that's your inclination (and why not invite the author?).

Not every aspect of the Brexit events and not every key character appears in "Brexit's A Musical Trick". Just as when selecting from Victor Hugo's masterpiece, it was necessary to concentrate on the core aspects of the psychodrama. Brexit has been described as "an argument in the Tory Party that got out of hand"; it has now fundamentally changed the Conservative Party to the extent that large numbers of Tory MPs and supporters no longer belong in that Party. There has been of course much collateral damage already from the Brexit conflict, but the musical has as its main focus the mostly-Tory Brexit psychodrama with the ambitions of the main characters and with all its twists, turns, impossible goals, deceit, broken promises, and the destructive conflict that resulted.
If you find that your favourite Brexit character has not made it into the musical you may still find a relevant song in the later part of this book.
We also acknowledge a few anachronisms – Widdy Faragier represents Faragier's associates for example, but at a point in time earlier than you might expect. Sturgene's input has been focussed in the musical at a particular point in time.
Depending on the timing for any performance, many of the songs in the latter section of the Book ("Brexit's Still a Trick not a Treat") could be included in the final Act, or performed as encores. For example:

- We are Family (I've Not Got My Sister With Me)
- You Say 'Delay', And I'll Say 'We Go'.
- No-Deal Wizard
- Goodbye Speaker's Green Chair
- Any Deal Will Do
- You're A Pain, You Realise That Nobody Trusts You?
- Bercow's Yellow Hammer
- Somewhere the Dirt
- So Don't Go.
- Time Every Trade Deal (which would be an alternative ending).

You could also cut some songs if you wanted a shorter performance. Your audience will most probably remember some of the news, and be able to fill in any narrative gaps for themselves. Pick what you would like to sing, and enjoy it!

Brexit's Still a Trick not a Treat

September 2019

At the end of the book "Brexit's a Trick not a Treat?", we had reached the point at which the Government had involved the Queen in a 5-week prorogation of Parliament. The relevant cases went to the Supreme Court. The Government's position was challenged by Gina Miller together with interventions from Scotland, Wales and Northern Ireland, and Sir John Major, Baroness Chakrabarti and the Public Law Project.

The Supreme Court determined that the prorogation was unlawful, and prevented Parliament from exercising its duty of scrutiny without reasonable justification; the Prime Minister's opinion that David Cameron was a "girly swot" was not considered to be reasonable justification. The prorogation order which Black Rod had brandished had the legal effect of a blank piece of paper.

Go Now Go Boris

24 September 2019

Inspired by: *I Will Survive*

At first, we were concerned, was this justified?
Kept thinking Parliament should still be sitting with MPs inside.
And so we wrote so many words explaining how you did us wrong.
And we grew strong.
And to the Court we went along
And so they're back
From prorograte
We'll just walk in to find the Speaker
Who can organise our fate,
We should have realised Black Rod

Had nothing that should lock the door
Black Rod was holding only a blank paper,
And it really meant no more
Go now go, walk out the door
Just you resign now
Not in power any more
Weren't you the one who tried to bluster, bluff, and lie?
Do you think we'd crumble?
Did you think we'd lay down and die?

Oh no not us, we will survive.
Oh, as long as we can legislate, we know that we will thrive.
We've got sessions that are live.
And we've got scrutiny to give and we'll survive
We will survive, hey, hey.
It took all the strength we had to document our case.
For scrutiny of our new laws we all have a place.
And they spent so many nights with Bills that would be on the shelf
You think we'd cry?
But now we hold our heads up high.
And see Gina
Somebody new
She's not a chained up little person
 - she can see through you.
And so, you felt like dropping Bills
And just expect them all to go?
Well they're all back for consideration,
But we don't need you, you know.

Go now go, walk out the door.
Just you resign now -
Not in power any more.
Weren't you the one who tried to bluster, bluff and lie.

Do you think we'd crumble?
Did you think we'd lay down and die?
Oh no not us, we will survive.
Oh, as long as we can legislate, we know that we will thrive.
We've got sessions that are live.
And we've got scrutiny to give and we'll survive
We will survive, hey, hey.

(Repeat last verse).

THE MORAL:
Oh, what a tangled web we weave between
When first we practise to deceive the queen.

Yellowhammer, Kingfisher and Black Swan

26 September 2019

"Yellowhammer" scenario when leaked was the "Base Case", but by the time the official version was published the Tipp-Ex had been duly wielded so that it was now supposedly the "Reasonable Worst Case".

When questioned the Gove seemed to stammer
About changing dates (Yellowhammer).
My guess is that he will not wish a
Need to encounter Kingfisher,
But all semblance of order is gone
If Brexit results in Black Swan.
We're mostly discussing the first;
A base case when written, not worst.

We are Family (I've not got my Sister with me)

27 September 2019

Inspired by: *We Are Family*

Following the resignation of Boris Johnson's brother Jo from the Cabinet, his sister Rachel questioned Boris Johnson's motives. A further line in this piece was amended after Boris Johnson's father also raised his doubts.

We are family. I've not got my sister with me.
We are family. Get out and let's leave the EC.

We are family. I've not got my brother with me.
We are family. Get out and let's leave the EC.

Everyone can see we're united. Or maybe not, but why?
When I speak, I get so excited, I might tell a lie.

All of the people around us they say, Can they be opposed?
Just let me state for the record, Parliament was better closed.

We are family. I've not got my MPs with me.
We are family. Get out and let's leave the EC. (sing it to me).

We are family. I've not got my country with me.
We are family. Get out and let's leave the EC.

Crashing out is fun and we've just begun.
To get our share from shorting the pound.
Hopes from our hackers and backers.
What goes round comes round.
No, we don't get depressed.
Here's what we call our exit door.
Have faith we'll leave on the thirty-first.
We won't tell you our plan but,
We won't break the Law

We are family. I've not got my sister with me.
We are family. Get out and let's leave the EC.

We are family. I've not got my brother with me.
We are family. Get out and let's leave the EC.

We are family (I've not got my father with me).
I've not got my MPs with me.
We are family. Get out and let's leave the EC.
(Get up and sing it to me).

We are family. I've not got my country with me (we're having fun).
We are family. Get out and let's leave the EC.

Get up, Get up, Get up and sing it to me.
Oh, I can't hear you y'all.
Oh, have faith in me and mendacity. Hey hey, oh hey hey hey.
Get out, get out y'all. Oh, hey hey hey.

I got my Geoffrey with me. Everybody, hey hey hey.
Get up, Get up and sing it to me.
Crash out is fun. Life, life has just begun for me.
I got my Priti with me.
Get up, Get up and sing it. Sing it, sing it, sing it, sing it to me.
Yeah, I'm Prime Minister, though that is sinister.
Get out, come on y'all.

We are family (yeah, sing it to me). I got Dom'nic Cummings with me.
We are family (yeah). Get out and let's leave the EC.
(Get up and sing it to me).

We are family (we're having lots of fun now).

I got all my money with me (Get up and sing it sing it to me).
We are family (yeah).
Get out and let's leave the EC.

We are family. I've not got my sister with me.
We are family (we're family). Get out and let's leave the EC.

We are family. I've not got my brother with me.
We are family (I got no sister with me).
Get out and let's leave the EC.

We are family. I've not got my father with me
We are family (we're family). Get out and let's leave the EC.

We are family. I've not got my MPs with me
We are family (we're family). Get out and let's leave the EC.

We are family. I've not got my Party with me.
We are family (we're family). Get out and let's leave the EC.

We are family. I've not got my country with me.
We are family (I got no sister with me).Get out and let's leave the EC.

We are family. I've not got my sister with me
We are family (we're family). Get out and let's leave the EC.

We are family. I've not got my brother with me
We are family (we're family). Get out and let's leave the EC.

Constitutional Lessons from Eton

September 2019

Boris Johnson was criticised for not properly recognising the British constitution,

So, what could he do, with the heat on?
In Parliament he has been beaten;
- Undertake, if he's keen,
As indeed did the Queen,
Constitutional lessons from Eton.

A sigh of relief I would heave

29 September 2019

I posted the following, and speculated that the Opposition might need to remove the Government with a Vote of No Confidence:
"Dominic Grieve has shown, is showing and will surely continue to show good judgement, decisiveness, determination, knowledge, clarity, intelligence, empathy, morality, calmness, and courage - in short, leadership. He would be the ideal candidate for a temporary Prime Minister".

Whether we Remain or we Leave,
A sigh of relief I would heave,
For judgement and clarity,
Sense and morality,
If PM was Dominic Grieve.

Model of Restraint

30 September 2019

The Prime Minister described himself as being "the model of restraint". He denied any conflict of interest in the awarding of Government grants and presence on trade trips for his friend Jennifer Arcuri.

I believe that there's been some complaint
That I am a liar; I ain't.
Alleging some conflict
Of interest? - you're con-tricked
The model, that's me, of restraint".

I build bridges to those on their side,
Though it helps to have some place to hide.
I support scrutiny -
Just don't do it to me!
And please don't ask me why I lied.

Will you Subpoena Obama ?

3 October 2019

Inspired by: *Do You Like Pina Colada?*

President Trump had pressurised the Ukraine government to investigate the son of his electoral opponent Joe Biden, using the potential of withdrawing US state aid to Ukraine as a lever.

This became the subject of impeachment hearings for the President.

Will you subpoena Obama?
Were you caught in Ukraine?
D'you ask leader Zelensky?
Now you may not explain.
But you asked his attorney,
Can Biden be hurt?
And what happened in China?
Is there any more dirt?

And then "Biden Corruption"
Was the name of your ad.
'Cos you attacked Hunter,
So you'd damage his Dad
That's the Biden you're facing,
Seems you're scared of him now
CNN wouldn't air it,
Your account of the row.

Yes you are meaner, no charmer;
We can see that is plain.
You're not into impeachment.
And you say there's no stain.
But they're hearing from Volker.
Who can tell of your sin.
He was working with Russia,
And he you may dob you in.

So Rudi Guiliani
Evidence would amass.
For his investigation
Into their natural gas.
Well he didn't go looking -
Found Ukraine on the map.
And he said that the scandal
Just arrived in his lap.

Will you subpoena Obama?
Were you caught in Ukraine?
Do you fancy impeachment,
Seeing Mueller again?
If you like tweeting at midnight,
So that everyone jumps,
Then you'll insult the leaders,
But you will come up Trump's.

Will you subpoena Obama?
Were you caught in Ukraine?
Do you fancy impeachment,
Seeing Mueller again?
If you like tweeting at midnight,
So that everyone jumps,
Then you'll insult the leaders,
But you will come up Trump's.

Horse to Talk

4 October 2019

Boris Johnson had been given 30 days by Angela Merkel to come up with a revised Deal, but there was little sign of any activity until the Benn Act sought to outlaw 'No Deal".

A man was condemned once to die,
And so, to the gallows did walk.
But said to the king "Please can I
Now teach your old horse to talk?
If I can do that in a year,
Would you then let me go free?
Do you think my request is fair, sir?"
And the King said, "This I must see".

"But a year's what you'll have – no more time.
To resolve this remarkable matter.
Then you'll be absolved of your crime,
Provided I hear my horse chatter".
The man's friends said, "Now what have you done?
Your state's not improved one iota.
The King, who's expecting some fun,
Won't be pleased to find you are a joker".

"Not so", said the man to his friends,
"I think I can safely demur.
Consider four ways that this ends
In my favour within the next year.
By the time that 12 months have gone by,
The King, who does not sound too well,
Might, by then, have occasion to die,
Saving me by the royal death knell".

"I understand well why you ask.
You think in a year I'll have fluffed it.
You think that I'll fail at this task.
But maybe by then I'll have snuffed it.
There are other chances of course,
Which provide me a way through this strife;
Consider the death of the horse,
Extending my options of life".

"Three ways" said the friends, "And no more".
"There's a lot can take place in a year.
But you said your escape routes were four.
Is there anything else could occur?"

"Consider who might be my saviour;
Another way that my luck rises -
An outcome that's all in my favour -
The horse might just talk, and surprise us".

So, Boris now, how is he coping
With any plans that he devises?
He's lunching with Juncker and hoping
The horse might just talk, and surprise us.

Inspired by: *The Horse to Talk fable*

The horse talked – by abandoning the temporary backstop in favour of a permanent arrangement previously rejected by the UK.

Effortless Superiority

6 October 2019

Responding to story: "Boris Johnson's Brexit plan shows 'blatant disregard for people and businesses in Northern Ireland' say party leaders in joint letter" – Belfast Telegraph.

Eton seeks to imbue their minority,
"Effortless superiority".
All Boris could do
Was one out of two,
But he could not achieve the majority.

Boris and Hungary

6 October 2019

One theory about the Government's Cummings Plan was that they would request an extension to EU membership as required by the Benn Act but would ask Hungary to veto the extension. Suspicions were raised when Hungarian diplomats visited 10 Downing Street.

"Boris Johnson hopes Hungary will veto Britain's potential request for a Brexit delay, according to reports" – headline on Politics Home

So, Boris still flees from his blunders,
Naturally though one still wonders
If he makes us angry,
In dealing with Hungary
Will their invoice be paid by his funders?

You Say Delay, and I'll say We go

Inspired by: *You say Goodbye, and I Say Hello*

6 October 2019

Boris Johnson released a statement to clarify his position

You say "Benn".
I say "Go".
You say "Stay"
But I say
"Go, go, go."

Oh no.
You say "Delay".
And I'll say "We go."
"We go, we go."
I don't know why
I'd say "I'll die",
I'll say "We go."
"We go, we go."
I don't know why
I'd say "Delay",
I'll say "We go."

I'll say, "Stay",
I'll say, "Go",
I'll say, "Stay"
And I'll say,
"Go, go, go".

Oh no!
I'll say, "Goodbye",
And I'll say, "We go",

"We go, we go,"
I don't know why
I'd say, "I'd die",
I'll say, " We go,
We go, We go"
I'll toe the line.
I'll say I'll sign.
I'll say, " We go ".

Why, why, why,
why, why, why,
Do I say,
"Goodbye, goodbye",
"Bye, bye, bye bye"?

Oh no.
I'll say, "I'll die",
And who'll say, "Veto,"?
"Veto, veto".
I'll toe the line,
I'll say "I'll sign",
Who'll say, "Veto,"?
"Veto, veto"
Now I know why
I'll say, "I'll sign",
Who'll say, "Veto"?

I'll say, "Yes",
I'll say, "No".
I'll say, "Stay",
And I'll say,
"Go, go, go",

Oh, oh no.
I'll say, "Goodbye",
And who'll say, "Veto"?
"Veto, veto."
Now I know why
I will obey,
Who'll say, "Veto"?
"Veto, veto".
I don't know who
It is will say,
Will say, "Veto".
"Veto, veto"?
Now I know why
I'd say, "I'll sign",
I'll say, "We go wow,
oh we go".
"We go"
Hey hey, yellowhammer,
Hungery, yellowhammer,
Hey hey, yellowhammer,
Hungary, yellowhammer,
Hey hey, and kingfisher,
Black Swan, and kingfisher,
Black Swan and kingfisher,
Black Swans, kingfisher.

(It turns out that this was his original briefing to the Scottish Court yesterday, but the solicitor did not pass it on verbatim).
Hope that clears everything up.

No-Deal Wizard

7 October 2019

Inspired by: *Pinball Wizard*

The Government insisted that the UK would definitely leave the EU on 31st October, and refused to say how this would be done, because the "Benn Act" sought to prevent this.

This resulted in much speculation about their Cunning Plan to achieve a No Deal departure. The Prime Minister was very confident of this, and so there had to be a twist!

Ever since he was a writer
He's played the silly fool.
He thinks he is a fighter.
He won't obey a rule.
Some girls think he's not bad.
But some think he's a tool.
That bluff dumb and blond cad
Sure plays a silly fool.

He's been quite a breeder.
Thinks he's good at chat,
Stood as Tory leader.
Said he could use GATT;
Likes to think last minute;
And Tories think he's cool.
That bluff dumb and blond cad
Sure plays a silly fool.

He's a No Deal spinner.
There has to be a twist.
A No Deal spinner
Will obey just the gist.

How do you think he's leaving?
I don't know!
What lets him escape?

There may be revisions
When he moves his lips.
He creates divisions
But he'll take the Whips.
Unicorns we've not had -
A cone upon a mule.
That bluff dumb and blond cad
Sure plays a silly fool.

He thought he had
A deal at a cinch.
But he just showed
We can't trust him one inch.

Has he ever confessed
When he helps his friends?
Not declared an interest
When the rules he bends?
And though he is an Ox grad,
Once of Eton school.
That bluff dumb and blond cad
Sure plays a silly fool.

The Cunning Plan turned out to be simply not signing the mandated letter that requested an extension, and sending another letter asking the EC to ignore the mandated letter. This Cunning Plan didn't work
Millions of pounds were wasted on planning for a No Deal that was dependent on the Cunning Plan working.

Goodbye Speaker's Green Chair

8 October 2019

Inspired by: *Goodbye Yellow Brick Road*

Speaker John Bercow bade farewell to the Speaker's Chair after a colourful career in which he was not afraid to berate MPs such as Geoffrey Cox if they infringed Commons rules or courtesies.

Some commentators criticised his readiness to respond to the will of the members of the House of Commons.

When are you going to calm down?
When are you going to learn?
You should have stayed at your box,
Not perambulate Cox with your turn.

You know that I'm no Tory stooge now.
The backbenchers do have a view.
I'm not a servant for the PM to order,
This boy owes nothing to no-one - that's true - ue, -ue
Orrder, order! Or-order!

So goodbye Speaker's green chair,
Where I've aimed to fulfil my true role.
You can't stop me from progressing.
I'm done with keeping control.

I don't give a flying flamingo
Whether you think that I'm fair.
Oh, I've finally decided my future lies.
Beyond the Speaker's green chair – air -air.
Orrder, order! Or-order!

What do you think will happen?
How long will Prime Minister reign?

Maybe you're going to need a new referendum,
To choose between Leave and Remain.

Maybe you'll get a replacement;
There's many out there who'll be fair.
Clear heads who won't stand no nonsense
Calling the Members to book - from the Chair – air -air.
Orrder, order! Or-order!

So goodbye Speaker's green chair.
As I've got to get on with my life.
You can't blame me for the car sign;
The car belongs to my wife.

Back I will go to my own family
Children and Sally so fair.
Oh, I've finally decided my future lies
Beyond the Speaker's green chair – air -air.
Orrder, order! Or-order! Ah.

Any Deal Will Do

13 October 2019

Inspired by: *Any Dream Will Do*

The Government continued to insist that they would not break the law but that the UK would definitely leave the EU on 31st October, and refused to say how this would be done, bearing in mind that the "Benn Act" sought to prevent this. This resulted in much speculation about their Cunning Plan. One theory was that they would put a Deal to Parliament, get it passed, thus meeting a criterion of the Benn Act, but then fail to implement it, triggering a No-Deal exit from the EU – and so "Any Deal Will Do".

This may have been the intention. In fact, such a course of action was forestalled by an amendment proposed by Sir Oliver Letwin and passed just as People's Vote marchers came into Parliament Square. The amendment withheld Commons approval for the revised Withdrawal Agreement until after the "Benn Act" deadline of 19th October, thus requiring the Prime Minister to ask for an extension. Certainly, there appeared to be no other plan, other than the stunt of sending the letter as required but failing to sign it, and sending another letter (signed) contradicting the letter mandated by the Benn Act. This stunt was pointless; the EU responded to the (unsigned) letter which had been mandated by Parliament.

Speculation has since then grown as to whether the Conservative Government has other plans to achieve a No Deal Brexit at the end of 2020.

I closed my mind, and sent an order -
Just fix the border, satisfy EU.
Those Customs Posts just get us flustered –
We don't want them busted.
Any Deal will do.

Leo Varad- kar, Simon Coveney -
They are the only Irish folk I knew.
But them and me, we saw a pathway;
So, we got halfway -
Any Deal will do.

A flash of smiles, we close the files,
My golden locks, they hide my wiles,
The tariffs faded into rebates.
Ulster left alone.

I closed my mind, and thought election.
Farage rejection, here's my plan that's new.
The Parliament, it will be waiting,
Still hesitating,
Any Deal will do.

A flash of lips, I make some quips,
I book the ships, I trust the Whips,
The rebels fading into lost votes.
I'm not left alone?

And in the House, I will promote it
And let them vote it, so it goes through
In 2020, I won't complete it.
They'll say I cheated.
But No Deal's through.

Brexit Oddity

By Peter Cook

Inspired by: *Space Oddity*

Ground control to Boris J
Ground control to Boris J
Take your Coke and Whizz and put your bike away

Ground Control to Boris J
Commencing countdown, engines on
Check ignition and may Brexit be with you

This is Ground Control to Boris J
You've really made the grade
And the Tabloids want to know whose pants you wear
Now it's time to leave the EU if you dare

This is Boris J to Ground Control
I'm queuing at Dover
And I'm floating in a strong and stable way
And the stars look very different today

For here am I sitting in a white van
Far above the EU
The UK is royal blue
And there's nothing you can do

Though I'm past one hundred thousand miles
I'm feeling very still
And I think my spaceship knows which way to go
Tell Jezza I love him very much, he knows

Ground Control to Boris J
Your WAB is dead, there's something wrong

Can you hear me, Boris J? Can you hear me, Boris J?
Can you hear me, Boris J?

Here am I floating 'round my white van
Far above the moon
The UK is blue, and there's nothing I can do

Queens' Speech (Honest Version)

15 October 2019

Inspired by: *Torn*

The Queen's opinion on the speech she was required to read has not been published …. Until now!

I thought I saw a man sent to lead
He was warm,
He came to me like he was justified
He said he'd show them how to win
But he couldn't be that man they adored
I don't think he knows, or seem to care
What his brain is for
No, no one trusts him anymore
There's nothin' where he wouldn't lie
Negotiation has run dry
That's what's going on
Nothing's there but scorn
Ireland's out of faith
MPs how they feel!
Opposed and now unwhipped
Lying on the Commons floor
The promise never changed
Into a new Deal
Wide awake and I can see for his plans he has scorn.
He's a little late
And my speech is torn

You're a Pain, You Realise that Nobody Trusts You?

16 October 2019

Inspired by: *"You're So Vain"*.

The Prime Minister presented a programme for the new session of Parliament which could never be executed since he had created a situation in which he had a very substantial minority

You wrote stuff several years ago,
There's all your lies for the Telegraph.
Well you said that bananas couldn't curve,
Led your fans up the garden path.
But you gave away your heart and soul, and
Led Leave gang for a laugh.
We had some dreams but there's clouds in the offing,
Clouds in the offing,
And you're a pain.
You realise that nobody trusts you?
You're a pain (you're a pain).
I bet you know that nobody trusts you,
Don't you? Don't you?

Well I hear you saw Leo Varadkar,
Who was smiling when you begun;
And Merkel, Barnier, also Juncker,
On having two borders, not one.
Well no bridge over double borders can fix
The stitch-up that you have done.
Wrote a Queen's Speech,
but it's fantasy programme,
Fantasy programme, and
You're a pain.
You realise that nobody trusts you?

You're a pain (you're a pain).
I bet you know that nobody trusts you,
Don't you? Don't you? Don't you?
(instrumental)
You wrote a speech but it's fantasy programme,
Fantasy programme
And
You're a pain.
You realise that nobody trusts you?
You're a pain (you're a pain).
You realise that nobody trusts you,
Don't you? Don't you?

Well I know you'll go to Parliament,
Telling them you've got a Deal,
Saying that you are seeking their principled votes,
And that implementation is real.
But you'd leave it until Halloween,
And let time work a repeal.
Everyone knows that you're
Caught by the Benn Act
Caught by the Benn Act, and
You're a pain
You realise that nobody trusts you?
You're a pain (you're a pain)
I bet you know that nobody trusts you?
Don't you? Don't you? Don't you?
(instrumental)

You say some words but
We never can trust you,
Never can trust you.
And you're a pain.

You realise that nobody trusts you.
You're a pain (you're a pain).
You realise that nobody trusts you
Don't you?

If you are singing this to a karaoke track, then you may need to vary how much you repeat chorus lines, depending on which karaoke track you use, but it should fit if you adjust the number of chorus repeats to the track

Bercow's Yellow Hammer

By Peter Cook

Inspired by: *Maxwell's Silver Hammer*

Bercow's quizzical, studied what's admissible
Process in the House
Late nights all aglow in the Commons
Oh, Berc – o – ow

Death-Knell Johnson-Lies, all eyes on the Hedge Fund prize
Calls him on the phone
Can I take you out of the picture?
Oh, Berc – o – ow

As Brexit's getting ready to go
A knockout we can't ignore:

Bang! Bang! Bercow's Yellowhammer comes down upon our head
Bang! Bang! Bercow's Yellowhammer makes sure that Brexit's dead.

Back in Number Ten Johnson plays the fool again
Cummings gets annoyed
Wishing to create an unpleasant Sce, e, e, ene

He tells him to say Yellowhammer's not Doomsday
So he fakes and lies
Lying fifty times: "No Deal isn't So, o, o, o"

He turns his back on democracy. Grieve comes up from behind

Bang! Bang! Bercow's Yellowhammer comes down upon our head
Bang! Bang! Bercow's Yellowhammer makes sure that Brexit's dead.

Scottish Judges say, "We caught a dirty one" Johnson stands alone
Painting testimonial busses Oh, oh, oh, oh

Mogg and Kate Hoey, screaming to the gallery
Say he must be free (Johnson must be free)
The judges don't agree and they tell him So, o, o, o

But as the ruling's leaving their court A noise comes from behind

Bang! Bang! Bercow's Yellowhammer comes down upon our head
Bang! Bang! Bercow's Yellowhammer makes sure that Brexit's dead.
Whoa, oh, oh, oh

Yellowhammer man

Everyone Wants to Get Brexit Done

22 October 2019

Inspired by: "*I'd like to teach the world to sing*", *although the parody version below has more verses.*

Sometimes people feel that these songs show some favour to the Remain. To provide some balance, here is some support for the Government position.

For simplicity we have kept the same structure for each verse, with some optional "verse afterthought lines such as "That's the line I take". If you are singing this version, sing the same tune for each verse, other than any "extra" last lines.

The Government tells us that "Everyone wants to get Brexit done".

They'd like us to get Brexit done;
It doesn't matter how.
They'd back our plan if we had one.
They'd like it finished now.

I'm glad we found they all want this;
Ignore the latest polls.
In fact, please give all polls a miss
If they don't match our goals.

I'm glad it is the People's Wish -
I'm sure that's what they mean.
And never mind the farms and fish;
We'll leave on Halloween.
(That's the line I take).

A million seemed a bit unsure ??
In London had a trek.?
I guess they're not sure we'll endure,
And came here just to check.
La- la -la- la-la, Oo-oo-oo-oo-oo

Euro elections favoured Leave,
Except where that's not true.
Though those #DeniedMyVote did grieve.
Don't worry - that's not you.

And here's the thing that you should say,
Before you go to bed.
"I do believe in Brexit, - hey!"
Else unicorns are dead
(yes they all are dead).

They're happy if we base our plans
On WTO.
It will be backed by all our fans,
Like on that "This Week" show.
(When the Leave bombed so)[1]

I'd like to teach MPs to vote
In perfect harmony.
You want to see what else I wrote?
Not in this company.

And Benn wrote letter we must send,
Which we don't think he meant.
My signature's not at the end -
And see what else I've sent.

---

[1] I bumped into Sam Gyimah on the People's Vote March, and gave him a copy of "Brexit's a Trick Not a Treat?". We also talked about the "This Week" show where Sam was a guest and Hard Brexiteer James Delingpole's argument fell apart under questioning by Andrew Neill (as recognised by James D, who acknowledged at the end that he had no answer to the questions).

So let us leave the EU when
This month hits thirty-one.
You will not hear of Brexit then,
As Brexit will be done.

In sunlit uplands we'll succeed,
With nothing more to do.
We'll have achieved our greatest need;
We will have left EU.

So Where it is, Merry Brexit?

25 October 2019

Inspired by: *So Here it is Merry Christmas*

The Withdrawal Bill secured Second Reading by thirty votes, but a rushed timetable was not supported. Boris Johnson chose not to have any further debate on the Bill and called for a General Election

Are you hanging on oh Johnson on your Deal?
It's the time when every Party makes a meal.
Do you believe in full Withdrawal?
For election do you call?
Do the MPs vote – need two-thirds of them all!
So where it is, Merry Brexit?
Everybody has got one
Look to the Trade Deals
It's only just begun.

Are you wary of the elephant in the room?
The Tusk and Barnier but you'll have no gloom?
Does the Corbyn always tell ya
That some fear deselection
But he'll finally help you to your own election.

Are you hanging on oh Johnson on your Deal?
Did you think that win by thirty seemed so real?
Do you think this is your luck's ridge?
Will you dangle from a truss bridge?
Do you think that you're safe in Uxbridge?

The Twelfth of Never for Brexit

29 October 2019

Inspired by: *The Twelfth of Never*

A General Election was called for December 12th

You ask me how long for Brexit, must I explain?
The reasons we can't Brexit, we find time and again.
You'll try one more election, like Theresa thought she'd do.
Until the 12th of never we'll still try to leave EU.

Hold the vote, let's have one more go.
Hold the vote, December time in winter snow.

We'll argue till the Leavers decide a deal;
We'll argue till the leaders have lost their appeal;
We'll argue till we've worn down all reasonable folk,
Until the 12th of Never, or until #Revoke.
Until the 12th of Never, or until #Revoke.

The Twelve Lies of Tories

2 November 2019

Inspired by: *The Twelve Days of Christmas*

A full list was included on the Labour website with full references in each case for the lie and for the truth of the matter.

Now the first lie of Tories that Boris said to me
Was a real fudge in the Irish Sea.

The second lie of Tories that Boris said to me
Deal passed in Commons,
And a real fudge in the Irish Sea.

The third lie of Tories that Boris said to me,
A great new Deal,
Deal passed in Commons,
And a real fudge in the Irish Sea.

The fourth lie of Tories that Boris said to me,
Billion a month cost,
A great new Deal,
Deal passed in Commons,
And a real fudge in the Irish Sea.

The fifth lie of Tories that Boris said to me,
For- ty hos- pit- als,
Billion a month cost,
A great new Deal,
Deal passed in Commons,
And a real fudge in the Irish Sea
The sixth lie of Tories that Boris said to me,
Health three billions,
For- ty hos- pit- als,

Billion a month cost,
A great new Deal,
Deal passed in Commons,
And a real fudge in the Irish Sea.

The seventh lie of Tories that Boris said to me,
Levelled up school funding,
Health three three billions,
For- ty hos- pit- als,
Billion a month cost,
A great new Deal,
Deal passed in Commons,
And a real fudge in the Irish Sea.

The eighth lie of Tories that Boris said to me,
Ending London homeless,
Levelled up school funding,
Health three three billions,
For- ty hos- pit- als,
Billion a month cost,
A great new Deal,
Deal passed in Commons,
And a real fudge in the Irish Sea.

The twelfth lie of Tories that Boris said to me,
Lies about Labour, We won't repeat them,
Lies about Labour, We won't repeat them,
Ending London homeless,
Levelled up school funding,
Health three three billions,
For- ty hos- pit- als,
Billion a month cost,
A great new Deal,
Deal passed in Commons, And a real fudge in the Irish Sea.

As Smart as Farage?

12 November 2019

Nigel Farage withdrew Brexit Party candidates where they were competing with current Tory MPs, in a move to avoid splitting the Hard Brexit vote.

Farage with noble arbitrage,
Has decided against sabotage.
The question for Corbyn
And also for Swinson:
Are you just as smart as Farage?

Subsequent events may indicate that the answer to this question was "No".

Somewhere the Dirt

6 November 2019

Inspired by: *Somewhere My Love (popularised in the film "Dr Zhivago")*

The report on Russian interference in the 2016 referendum was not published because the Prime Minister refused to sign it off even after all security clearance had been completed.

Somewhere the dirt, is resting in this thing,
Although the hurt, will not be seen till Spring.
Somewhere the bill, glistens with stolen gold,
And there are dreams, nightmares we won't be told.
Some way, they flashed their roubles too,
Some day, whenever Putin breaks through.
We'll see report, after election's won.
MPs denied, until the deed is done.
Till then, oh Gove, keep up the plot to Leave,
With a No Deal, but don't tell Mr Grieve.

Tories are Sending Lies to me,

20 November 2019

Inspired by: *Momma, he's making eyes at me.* See the Lena Zavarone version.

Actions which unbelievably were defended by the Chairman of the Conservative party and Cabinet members included breaking Twitter rules to masquerade as an independent fact-checking site, and doctoring a video of Keir Starmer to make it look as if he had no response to a question about Brexit. The Conservative Party were warned by Twitter that any further misuse would result in sanctions by Twitter.

(The day after this was written, the Conservative Party created a fake "Labour Party manifesto" site, and paid for Google advertising in order that people searching for the Labour Party manifesto find the fake site first).

Tories are sending lies to me,
Tories, who are not nice to me,
Tories, they're almost breaking my heart.
They've lost their way, Mercy!
Where's their conscience gone then?

Tories, they want to Brexit me, and hurt economy.
Please don't think that I am bitter,
They're pretending on their Twitter,
Tories, not fooling me.

Tories are sending lies to me,
Tories, think we will rise, you see,
Tories, they're always breaking the rules
They've lost their way, Mercy!
Where's their conscience gone then?

Tories, they want to Brexit me, and hurt economy.
They said that they were just hearty
When they're bribing Brexit Party,
Tories, not fooling me.

Tories are sending lies to me,
Tories, think we're not wise, you see,
Tories, they're always breaking the rules
They've lost their way, Mercy!
Where's their conscience gone then?

Tories, they want to Brexit me, and hurt economy.
They said that it was no drama
When they took words from Keir Starmer
Tories, not fooling me.
Tories, not fooling me.

Trumping the NHS

Inspired by: *My Favourite Things*
28 November 2019

"The USA reserves the right to withdraw all trade, aid and communication upon the non-compliance of the UK to allow open discussions about the sale of all assets within and partnered with the National Health Service"

Assets included we'd like to see bartered:
All within NHS or that are partnered.
Open discussion that this outcome brings,
These are a few of our favourite things.

Access for traders that's quite comprehensive,
Patents extended so drugs are expensive,
Big pharma able to bring out big stings,
These are a few of our favourite things.

If the UK
Won't comply with,
All we want for trade,
We'll simply refuse to communicate, and
They'll wish that they ...had stayed.

Flexible Tories in no way reliant
On Green inclinations, just with us compliant.
Always respond when our telephone rings.
These are a few of our favourite things.

If we can't get
All we want from
Your great NHS,
We'll simply withdraw from the talks that you'll need
That's until you say "Yes".

So Don't Go

Inspired by: *Let it Go (from "Frozen")*

Boris Johnson (and Nigel Farage) declined to appear on the debate Channel 4 organised on climate change for Party Leaders. In their stead Channel 4 placed ice sculptures on the relevant podiums.

28 November 2019

Studio lights on Channel 4 tonight.
Not a Tory to be seen.
And I chose my isolation.
Just my Dad and Gove on the scene.

The ice is melting on that highlit podium.
But I couldn't go and cope with all that odium.
Don't waffle more, don't let them see.
Be the good guy not there, that's it for me.
Conceal, it's real but just don't go.
I'm for no-show.

So don't go, so don't go.
Can't say some stuff anymore.
So don't go, so don't go.
Go away, don't cross that door.
I don't care what Channel 4 will say.
Let the ice block melt.
I didn't want snowflake votes anyway.

So don't go, so don't go.
Can't say some stuff anymore.
So don't go, so don't go.
Go away don't cross that door

So don't go (go, go, go go, go go, go go, go, go, go go)
So don't go.

So don't go.
So don't go.

It's funny how Channel Four makes everything seem tough.
And I fear that they might ask me questions that are rough.
My Dad and Gove should be enough.
To waffle on with usual stuff.
No right, no wrong, no rules for me.
I'm free.

So don't go, so don't go.
Can't say some stuff anymore.
So don't go, so don't go.
Go away don't cross that door.
I don't care what Channel 4 will say.
Let the ice block melt.
I didn't want snowflake votes anyway.

My support's solid without my need of Channel Four.
I've got those votes secured from folk who are so sure.
I'll take back their licence, because they are not nice
How dare they replace me with a block of ice.

So don't go.
I didn't want snowflake votes anyway.
So don't go, so don't go.
Though I'll get elected again.
So don't go, so don't go.
The perfect times have gone.
Here I stand as the Party planned.
Let the votes flow on.

Ode to Tactical Voting

10 December 2019

Inspired by: *Ode to Joy*

On that day we will be voting
Use vote well, support the truth.
Only true facts we'll be noting
When inside the polling booth.
Read no stories,
From the Tories,
They hope you won't realise
All is fiction, no constriction.
Full Fact Check tells us they're lies.

This is not a dinner party;
It's time to be practical.
Whether your support is hearty,
Your vote must be tactical.
Hope you chose now,
Hold your nose now,
If you're picking second choice.
Combination for the nation -
You've chosen to have a voice.

That's Why They Call Me Boris

Inspired by: *Monty Python Spanish Inquisition sketch*

BORIS JOHNSON:
I didn't expect a British Inquisition
But on the other hand NOBODY expects a British inquisition.

My one key weapon is **Bluff**. Unchallengeable bluff. Making out I don't know what's going on. Pretending that I have no idea about Tory fake websites and Tory Twitter scams. And **Obfuscation**. Ok, my two weapons are Bluff and Obfuscation. It doesn't matter what the question is, just throw in the Riddle of the Sphinx, Bermuda Triangle, one or two dead cats and Fermat's Last theorem, and everyone glazes over because none of them know what Fermat's Last Theorem is. Neither do I, but it does the trick. Then you can **Ridicule**. Oh yes, and Ridicule, that's another weapon.

Ok, my three key weapons are Bluff, Obfuscation, and Ridicule. Ridicule Jeremy Corbyn because he wants to ask the People what they want. What a crazy idea. Look what happened last time. Anyway we tried to implement it but Parliament wouldn't let me, and ended the debate. It's good to generate some **Indignation**, which is a key weapon. Look, I'll go out and come in again…

My four key weapons are Bluff , Obfuscation, Ridicule, and Indignation. Indignation at Parliament that stopped the debate on Brexit. If you use enough indignation then people won't spot that it was me that stopped the debate. By the way Interruption is quite a good weapon as well, but I think we've got enough weapons now. Except for **Silence**. Just don't go. Don't do the interview. Don't do the debate. Don't do the hustings. Then I can't say anything Stupid, which is my other key characteristic, but it's Trumped (see what I did there) by Silence. Silence wins.

So there we have it. Five key weapons. Bluff , Obfuscation, Ridicule, Indignation, and Silence, That's why they call me BORIS.

Brexit a Trick? – after the General Election

No Confidence

13 December 2019

The opportunity in early October to replace the Government with a Vote of No Confidence had not been pursued by the Opposition Parties. In the light of the General Election result, they might have cause to regret that.

Despite lack of Government competence,
And as Corbyn still sat on the fence,
To him and to Swinson:
"That's not how you win some.
You missed chance for Vote of No Confidence".

Proportional

14 December 2019

Turnout in the General Election was 67%.

I think we should lay the facts bare.
Say twenty-one voters are there.
Well six vote for Boris
But eight don't want Tories
And seven folk don't really care.

Time Every Trade Deal?

14 December 2019

Inspired by: *Climb Every Mountain*

Also inspired by many Remainers who conceded defeat online but also proposed a To Do list for the Prime Minister

Time ev'ry Trade Deal,
Forty to go
One a week by Autumn,
Should be fine, you know,

And sort out Ireland.
Trade checks it seems.
Implement some systems
If you want your dream.

A dream that will need
All the laws you can make
As you now have to lead,
So that you'll eat your cake.

And sort out Scotland.
They're a bit miffed.
You had better go there,
So there is no rift.

This rift is a risk,
If you drag them away
From EU Deal we had,
Towards Trump's USA.

Investors have fled.
You'll get them back?.
Usually it's lying.

That gets you the sack.

In fact we'd like this:
Lie a bit less.
Nurses that are real
Help the NHS.

You're in Our Hearts, It Must be Told

15 December 2019

Inspired by: *You're In My Heart*

Also inspired by Terry Reintke of the German Green Party seeking to set up a UK Friendship Group in the European Parliament.

I still can recall what year it was
When we joined up with EU.
Some benefits unnoticed.
We've said goodbye too soon.

Pleasing through the decades since,
Seeing gains that were astronomic.
I really must confess back then
The attraction was quite economic.

We took all those differences
That in the beginning were hard to accept.
And Euro crises, food excesses.
But we worked with experience.

The American leader with the bad soundbites.
Who tried to change our point of view.
His late night tweets were aimed at us.
but our hearts cried out for EU.

Chorus:
You're in our hearts, it must be told.
I thought we'd stay as I grew old.
You are our partners, you're our best friends.
You're in my soul.

Our love for you is immeasurable.
Our respect for you immense.
You're patient, respectful, and transparent.
Your Parliament makes sense.

You're a union, a friendship group.
You're a forum and a team.
You're the greatest group of nations here
Though some Brits play on a different theme

(Chorus)
You're a lesson in expansion
Please pardon the scansion
But here's peace and teamwork seen.
You're Gallic, Romantic, some beside Atlantic
We're the best team that's ever been

And there have been many deceits
Said by those who thought we'd Leave
We thought we'd Remain, but sadly it's plain
There were some who did the lies believe
(Chorus) – 3 times

Tombstone

It was suggested that Remainers might keep quiet about having voted for Remain. I suggested this for my tombstone.....

Here is where you lay me
At the end of my Campaign.
But for Brexit do not blame me.
For I voted to Remain.

Reference

Using the indexes

Have you ever been in a "Now where was that song?" moment? It can be tricky.

So, we have two indexes for the song-titles as in this book:

- One index for the musical
- And the second index for the other songs.

And then, in the case of the parody songs, we have more indexes, so that you can look the song up by the original title. Once again, we have

- One index for the musical
- And the second index for the other songs.

Where there is no obvious title (e.g. the song in its original form is just part of a track), then we have generally taken the first line as an effective title.

Index of song titles in the Musical[2]

[2] Images in the Index by OpenClipart-Vectors from Pixabay

Index of titles (excluding the Musical)

Index of references to original songs from our Musical

Index of references to original songs (excluding our Musical)

Do you need a speaker for your event?

The Art of Comic Song Parody

A lively exploration of the challenges of comic parody song, illustrated by audience's favourites and/or references to songs from "Brexit's a Treat not a Trick?" / "Brexit's a Musical Trick" / "I Don't Beg Pardon" (which might be audience favourites!) Mike discusses some principles of the emotional tone of the parody, as well as exploring the practical task for the parody poet. And of course, we hope you will join in a sing-song of some favourites,

Parody Creation – interactive workshop

After a brief exploration of principles, volunteers – or everyone – can help to create their own comic parody song with Mike's guidance, working in small or large groups. The result can be your copyright property when written.
Of course the results should then be sing together.

Viewdelta Press and Charity

Viewdelta Press has made the commitment that Viewdelta's net profit (including Mike's author's royalty) from the "Brexit" books will be donated to UK registered charities.

One way in which we do this is to provide author copies of our books free of charge to charities to sell at their events; the production cost that Viewdelta Press has in effect donated is then counted as part of our profit contribution.

If you would like your charity to sell author copies of our books and to retain the full takings from the sale of the books, please get in touch via the website www.viewdelta.com

The "Brexit's A Musical Trick" Authors

MIKE CASHMAN
Mike Cashman writes serious and satirical items on Brexit and other topics. and his pieces have been widely shared and appreciated. The satirical works have been gathered together in book form in the "Brexit's a Trick" books.
Previously he worked in teaching, IT, project and programme management, and international development.
He blogs at viewdelta.blogspot.com
He is married with 4 children and 10 grand-children.

ROBIN WALLINGTON
Composer and conductor. Robin's splendid song "I am the Very Model of A Prejudiced Etonian" squeezed into "Brexit's a Trick not a Treat?" at the last minute, and there was no better way to highlight the relevant character in "Brexit's a Musical Trick". The recording of the song by Richard Suart (baritone) and Richard Black (piano) achieved 90,000 views on YouTube.

PETER COOK
Peter Cook is an Author, Business Consultant, Scientist, Musician, Anti-Brexit campaigner, who declares himself to be "Tragically an only twin." (Google it!)

"Brexit's A Trick Not A Treat?"

If you have enjoyed this book then will surely also enjoy "Brexit's A Trick Not A Treat?"

From the original "Brexitian Fantasy" right up to the controversial "Try a Yellow Hammer round the Whole Country", all of Brexit is here (and even a little of Trump). Theresa May hears "Don't Cry for Leave Now Theresa", Rees-Mogg takes you down to his place by the tower, and we can all sing along to "How do you solve a problem like our Brexit?". Boris Johnson reckons "I'll GATT by with a little help from my friends", and the strains of "Brexit Pie" tell us

> "Bye, bye, to our time with EC.
> We are leaving without grieving for the trashed currency.
> Them good old boys climb the leadership tree
> Saying 'Look what it's doing for me
> Look what it's doing for me'."

Football fans will recognize "Brexit's Coming Home (Three Lines in the Whip)".

Mike Cashman worked for an international development charity for six years, and saw first-hand the effects of the damage to sterling from the Brexit events. So, he asks:

> "If you hoped for a Brexit that's sweet
> As a cake you can have and can eat,
> Do you now realise
> The extent of the lies,
> And that Brexit's a trick, not a treat?"

Viewdelta net royalty earnings from this book will be donated to UK registered charities.

To find online content related to this book (e.g. song videos on YouTube), search using #BrexitsATrickNotATreat

We're All Over the Place Online

Here is how to find our online content.

Our hashtags for all online content are

#BrexitsATrickNotATreat

#BrexitsAMusicalTrick

web: **www.viewdelta.com**
If you want to contact us (e.g. to request a talk or a writing workshop, or to discuss a possible co-operation), please see the contact options on the website.
If you would like to comment on our published content (paperbacks etc) then we recommend using the Facebook pages.
Facebook:
"Brexit's a Trick not a Treat"
"Brexit's a Musical Trick"
"I Don't Beg Pardon"
"Covid 19 Musical"

Twitter: **@viewdelta**
YouTube Channels: "Brexit's a Trick not a Treat" , "I Don't Beg Pardon"

Blog (serious analysis): **www.viewdelta.blogspot.com**
This is a separate stream of more serious analysis, not in general referenced to the satirical songs, though you may detect some themes that run through this blog and some songs
Quora: Mike Cashman
Twitter account and Quora feed are for all subjects, not just Brexit.

On YouTube, Relevant to our books

You can find our content by searching with these hashtags

#BrexitsATrickNotATreat

#BrexitsAMusicalTrick

#IDontBegPardon

#Covid19Musical

Look out for

"Brexitian Fantasy"

"I am the Very Model of a Prejudiced Etonian"

"I Dreamed a Dream"

"How Do You Solve A Problem Like Our Brexit?"

"Onward Brexit No Dealers"

"Bridge Over Doubled Borders"

"Do You See the People March?"

"No Deal Wizard"

"Any Deal Will Do"

and many more.

Please search using the hashtags to see the latest posts

If you want to make an audio recording, we would be pleased to turn it into a video. Or, if you want to make a video of one of these songs, then we would be interested in hosting it on our YouTube channel "Brexit's a Trick not a Treat". Please contact us via the www.viewdelta.com website.

"I Don't Beg Pardon" – the following book and CD

(Covid 19 Musical)

We hope you will alos enjoy reading "I Don't Beg Pardon (I'm Talking B*ll*cks from the Rose Garden)"next. This title song is based on the Rose Garden "Tell All (Not Quite)" Press conference, but there were details omitted from that, so we thought it would be helpful if we included them.

Many of your favorite characters return, as Boris begins by considering who he would like to dispose of in "Boris has got a little list". The further adventures of this country's leader and his assistant are explored in this new book. A trip to Durham and Barnard Castle is examined in the title song and others. Of course, there is always a case for balance, and we have suggested some basis for mutual support in "Stand by Your Dom". And three familiar witches consider "When Shall We Three Tweet Again"

For further light relief, there are versions of nine Shakespeare plays, each cut down to a manageable size for lockdown.

The position of Mike Cashman as family bard has been challenged by Hilary Cashman with a Latin reflection on the importance of keeping agreements, by Fred Cashman with a delightful folk song "Barnard Castle – Dom's Ditty", and by Peter Cashman with some lockdown instructions "Stay in Your House or Flat". Peter Cook provides the lyrics of his chart sensation "Alo Vera" and his touring song "Got to Leave old Durham Town"

Viewdelta net royalty earnings / profits from this book will be donated to coronavirus charities.

"Brexit's a Musical Trick" concert performance CD.

During Summer 2020 the Viewdelta singers recorded 24 songs (and a poem) from the Musical "Brexit's a Musical Trick", including many famous tunes. This was recorded in a socially distanced manner, one singer at a time, and mixed to produce this unique recording.
On one CD you can enjoy all these songs – also available on USB.

ACT 1 (CAMERINE)

Do or Die?

We Know What We're Voting For

Hasty Referendum

What Have I Done?

Do You See The People March ?

One Day More at Chequers

On My Own

An agreement running to 585 pages

A Little Vote of Pain

ACT 2 (THERYLINE)

At the End of The Day We Have Need of a Leader

What Have We Here, Oh You Closet Remainer ?

Lovely Tax Breaks

Master of The Spiel

In My Life

A Poll Full of Votes

Labour People

One's Mascot

Leave and Remain – Led By Donkeys

ACT 3 (BORIS VALBORIS)

Bring Him In

Help Us Out

I Dreamed a Dream

Empty Houses, Empty Benches

There was a wise lady who tackled a lie

Who is this Man?

Ain't It A Laugh

Failure Doesn't Matter in the Past

"I Don't Beg Pardon" CD.

On one CD you can enjoy all these songs, together with 8 very short Lockdown Shakespearean playlets and a sketch "When Shall We Three Tweet Again?" . Also available on USB.

ACT ONE - PREPARATION

Boris Has Got a Little List

Stay in Your House or Flat

Ill with Covid

ACT TWO - EXPEDITION

The Ballad of Dom & Bojo

Barnard Castle, Dom's Ditty

I Don't Beg Pardon, I'm Talking ** from the Rose Garden

Stand By Your Dom

ACT THREE - PREVENTION

Things that Will Astonish You..

Man Up, Mask Up, Protect Another Life….

A Song of Idiotic Prejudice

Heroes, Just for One Day

ACT FOUR - DISTRACTION

Brexitian Fantasy

I'm Just a Girl who Can't Say Go…

Onward Brexit No-Dealers

Port-A-Loo

Britannia Waives the Rules

ACT FIVE - CONGESTION, REFLECTION, AND REWARD OF THE UNDESERVING

The Virus Cometh

The Archers Comment

Lords of Delight

Kent Convoy

Public Inquiry Nightmare

What Others Have Said About Our Parody Songs

'This book is a chance to howl in laughter instead of anger. A laser-like humorous side swipe at the Brexit madness.'

Lord Michael Cashman (no relation), on "Brexit's a Trick, Not a Treat?"

"The best thing to come out of Brexit "

Hugh Grant retweeting the YouTube video of "I am the very model of a prejudiced Etonian"

ValBoris dreams a dream of Brexit

Who'd have thought Brexit would so inspire the musical theatre world? After Brexit: The Musical and Now That's What I Call Brexit, another show is on the way. The author Mike Cashman will include the script in a sequel to his book of satirical verses, "Brexit's a Trick Not a Treat"? "The musical begins with ValBoris," he explains, "who is struggling under a great injustice because all his life he has not been Prime Minister."

Sunday Times, "Atticus" 27 October 2019

"Very Witty "

Dillie Keane, "Fascinating Aida"

Please write your own review so that more will enjoy this book

Amazon Reviews - "Brexit's A Trick Not A Treat?"

☆☆☆☆☆

Great book for Remainers or Leavers!

This very clever and amusing book is a welcome relief from all the misery of Brexit. Doesn't matter whether you are a Remainer or Leaver - just sing along and enjoy with friends and family!

☆☆☆☆☆

Sing-along with Brexit

If you have no idea what is going on, or want to live the happy days of Brexit chaos in musical form - this book is for you. It contains over 100 pages of adaptations of popular songs with witty lyrics for different stages of the Brexit chaos.

☆☆☆☆☆

Better to laugh than cry

Whatever your views on Brexit, it dominates the news agenda and demands a response. This book is a light-hearted and honest response to the travails of British politics since 2016. It cuts through the nonsense with playful lyrics to recognisable popular tunes. Sing along in your head (or our loud if you're feeling bold!)

Amazon Reviews - "Brexit's A Trick Not A Treat?"
(continued)

☆☆☆☆☆

Ideal Christmas gift!

Brilliant! A witty and entertaining book, this would make an ideal Christmas present for those 'hard to buy' for people. Takes some of the animosity out of the Brexit situation. Well done!

☆☆☆☆☆

You can't argue with the title!

Extremely inventive parody of the highest quality, which succeeds in delivering a serious message on this most significant issue of our times.

☆☆☆☆☆

Has you singing along

A fresh and enjoyable approach to Brexit. Very well written parodies of well-known songs that have you singing along.

☆☆☆☆☆

Superb

Very clever, very funny. A much-needed lighter take on Brexit. Highly recommended.

www.ingramcontent.com/pod-product-compliance
Lightning Source LLC
Chambersburg PA
CBHW052355060726
47592CB00020B/2255

* 9 7 8 1 9 1 6 2 4 8 6 3 2 *